The Fat Ass Guide to Hiking:

Yellowstone National Park

by

Pudgy Buffalo

PUDGY BUFFALO PRESS

Cover, book, and map designs by
Christina Myers

Front Cover Photo:
Old Faithful, Yellowstone National Park
© Christina Myers

First Edition: April 2012

www.fatassguides.com

Table of Contents

About This Fat Ass Guide

Not written by a Sherpa. Not written for a Sherpa. *The Fat Ass Guide to Hiking: Yellowstone National Park* is the quintessential guidebook for active chubsters, adventure lovers with less than Olympian capabilities, and darn near anyone interested in exploring the bountiful treasures of America's first national park, just not at the breakneck speeds set forth in other books.

On a recent summer road trip through America's outdoor wonders, I had the pleasure of hiking some of this country's most spectacular trails. A pleasure, but no small beans for a semi-active 30-something with a penchant for doughnuts. My trail compadres were diverse: a young lady with the rock-scrambling dexterity of a mountain goat, a marathon-running college athlete, a dietician for the federal government, a mom with uncompromising Alpine legs, and a three-year-old dynamo.

This ultimate mash-up of ages, lifestyles, and endurance levels consistently agreed upon one thing: our guidebooks lacked accurate skill level descriptions. Though well-researched, the books seemed assembled by a team of professional mountaineers headed for the summit of Mount Everest.

After too many close calls and outright dangerous advice (No, Mr. Ranger, scaling the sheer face of a cliff with a toddler strapped to your back isn't a kid-friendly hike!), I decided that it was high time for a guidebook that realistically grades hikes for the average person interested in enjoying the outdoors. Since the average person these days skews a bit on the pudgy side, this Fat Ass Guide could very well be the guide for you!

Bon Appehike!

Pudgy Buffalo

Hiking Basics

First Steps

So you decided to get your fat ass up and go for a hike. Good for you! There's nothing like a little fresh air to make you feel alive in a way that an old DVR rerun just can't deliver. Before you thunder out the door and spin into oblivion, remember that venturing into the wilds requires prudence and planning because by its very nature the wilderness is unpredictable. Sensible preparation will help you craft an awesome trip that'll bring you back in one big, happy piece.

★ **BE AWARE** and **BE PREPARED.** Being aware of your surroundings, knowing your gear, and understanding your abilities will do leaps and bounds to keep you out of harm's way and prepare you for challenges along the trail.

Get Real

Be realistic about your abilities. Your casual hike is not the time to suddenly get boot camp crazy. When hiking with others, be wary of getting caught up in group-think carelessness and bravado. Use common sense. If something sounds ridiculously dangerous, it probably is. Don't cave to pressure; instead, choose a hike that's your speed and your style.

DANGEROUSLY TRUE:

CALAMITY CANYON

Licensed trail guides from a respectable adventure company agree to take a group of fit hikers up a remote river canyon with a 4,500-foot (1,372 m) elevation gain. There is no trail. The guides expect the duration of the hike to be six hours though none of them had ever hiked the site before.

The group begins their trek while their family and friends travel downriver by boat, where they expect to meet up with the hikers later in the day. The meeting time comes and goes without any sign of the hikers. Nighttime falls. Worry wracks the waiting group. Why hadn't the hikers returned?

High up in the canyon wall, the hikers and their guides encounter unexpectedly difficult terrain. Dangerous climbing maneuvers without proper equipment are required to cross sheer rock faces, sending some hikers into full-blown panic attacks and tear-gushing mania; still, the group remains determined to summit the canyon wall. They urge each other on and reach the top of the canyon moments before sunset.

The group accepts the challenge of a return hike on unstable ground in the dark because they didn't plan for flashlights. They blindly traverse the rugged terrain, incurring deep lacerations and many painful contusions. At the bottom of the canyon, they hop into their boat and run whitewater rapids in the dark to reach their final destination. At the downriver meeting spot, they are finally reunited with their hysterical loved ones.

I was among the people waiting for the hikers that harrowing night, and I can tell you that it is but for a special grace that nobody in the hiking group died. When I first heard about the plans for the hike, everything about it screamed trouble, and I opted to stay behind.

In this Dangerously True scenario, you can see how quickly a bad idea was embraced with bravado, justified by group-think, and snowballed into an avalanche of risky decision making. The parameters of the hike were clearly beyond the skill level for this group who didn't want to admit their own limitations. The group set themselves up for injury by being ill-equipped to deal with potential challenges along the way.

Lunacy prevailed as the group cavalierly gambled with their own lives in order to reach their goal. The licensed trail guides compounded the problem by knowingly taking undue risk because they didn't want to disappoint their charges with failure. The guides got caught up in rationalizing their own underestimations.

You must trust your own instincts and keep yourself educated about the risks of your adventure. If you happen to find yourself in a tough situation, do not let fear paralyze your rational thought. Trail guides are usually well-trained professionals, but the ultimate responsibility of keeping yourself safe lies with YOU.

★ **LOOK LIKE A WEENIE, LIVE TO HAVE ANOTHER MARTINI.** The benefits of looking like a lazy sack of marshmallows by not embracing undue risk may very well be staying alive, remaining unscathed, and preserving your gene pool.

Buying An Out

In the age of instant communication and quick solutions, a disturbing mentality of buying an out is permeating the adventuring world. Many people are more apt to take unwarranted challenges these days because they believe that if they get into a rough spot, they can just punch up emergency services on their portable devices, flash their platinum credit card, and be airlifted to safety.

Novice adventurers may not realize that the remoteness of many wilderness areas in Yellowstone do not accommodate cell phone service, and rescue squads will not risk their lives in insurmountable conditions to save your fat ass, no matter your wealth.

Again, the ultimate responsibility of keeping yourself safe and getting yourself out of jams lies with YOU.

Make a Decision

Which Adventure?

A million aspirations lead hikers down the diverse trails of Yellowstone National Park. Some are looking for a reasonable physical challenge. Others want to explore new, distant landscapes. Families might be looking for kid-friendly strolls, while solitary hikers may be seeking natural inspirations and amazing vistas. Perhaps a desire to study wildlife or learn about the area's unique geology informs your choice of trail. Maybe you're looking to pair your hike with a camping or fishing adventure. And wouldn't we all just love an awesome post for our social media pages?

Consider your own personal hiking desires, and use this Fat Ass Guide to help you choose the perfect adventure. Each trail subheading contains valuable information in list format that highlights trail ease, attractions, and compatible hiking activities. Easy trails are labeled FAT ASS FRIENDLY while strenuous trails are labeled FORGET IT, FAT ASS.

Keep in mind factors such as seasonal restrictions, accessibility, group hike options (particularly in bear habitats), and frequency of use when selecting your ideal trail.

How To Calculate Hike Duration

Naismith's Rule helps calculate the length of time a person can expect to complete a hike. Named after Scottish mountaineer William W. Naismith, this rule advises that normal persons on normal terrain under normal circumstances allow 1 hour for every 3 miles (4.8 km) of forward hiking plus 1 hour for every 2,000 feet (610 m) of elevation gain. This rule does not account for breaks, sightseeing, or any other pit stops, so calculate accordingly. If you are particularly hefty, add a generous amount of time to the equation.

When hiking in a group, calculate the speed based on the slowest person. Remember, with every hike, *the slowest person sets the pace*. This is not negotiable, so choose your hiking companions wisely. Nobody wants to wait for stragglers to catch up nor be a straggler huffing and puffing to keep up with the group.

Evolving Systems - Stay Informed

The wilds are constantly evolving systems. Once you've chosen your adventure, verify trail accessibility at the closest ranger station to the trailhead. Don't assume that trail conditions remain constant, and don't assume that a trail will be just like it was the last time you hiked it. Perhaps heavy snowmelt has turned a small stream into a rapidly racing gusher, washed out a footbridge, and transformed a one-mile hike into a five-mile hike. In this Fat Ass Guide, each area heading details nearby ranger stations, visitor centers, and information stations where you may find important trail information.

Gear Up

Although it'd be great to simply roll out of bed and traipse about the world in snuggly toga, that's not a realistic strategy for hiking. You need to be outfitted with the proper clothing and the proper gear for the sport of hiking, the condition of the trailhead, the season of the year, and the projected weather forecast.

Dress in Layers

Whether you're hiking in hot or cold weather, layer up! The purpose of layering clothing is to **WICK**, **INSULATE**, and **PROTECT**. As you encounter environmental changes or variations in your hiking intensity, you'll be able to add and remove layers as needed.

LAYER 1 - **WICK**: The clothing layer closest to your body must draw moisture and perspiration away from your skin and keep you dry and comfortable. Forget cotton because when it gets wet, it stays wet, and dries super slowly. For your inner layer, choose lightweight shirts and leggings made of polyester and polypropylene because these materials effectively wick and expel wetness.

LAYER 2 - **INSULATE:** Your middle layer must create an insulating air pocket to help regulate your body temperature. Add a few different coverings to this layer to create multiple air pockets. In cooler temperatures, wool, fleece, and synthetic fabrics create warm air barriers to keep you toasty. Avoid cotton and down because they are bad insulators when wet. In warmer temperatures, feel refreshed in thin loose-fitting, light-toned garments that reflect heat.

LAYER 3 - **PROTECT**: Your outer layer must keep you dry and protected from wind, rain, snow, and other natural elements while allowing your perspiration to escape. Your outer layer should be a lightweight waterproof shell that is also sturdy. Your shell should contain vents that allow for an outflow of your body's natural moisture.

Shoes and Socks

SHOES: Choose your hiking shoes wisely to avoid unnecessary pain and blisters. Athletic shoes with a durable sole are suitable choices for paved trails, boardwalks, and easily traversable paths with few geographical challenges. In this book, easy trails are marked FAT ASS FRIENDLY. For moderate trails, including trails with loose stones, lightweight ankle-high boots made from breathable fabrics with substantial traction on the sole are a great choice. The boots should support your ankles while keeping you mobile. Whichever shoes you choose, take them for a trial run before your hike, so you can make sure they are comfortable. You don't want to find out on the trail that your shoes are torture devices.

SOCKS: Avoid cotton socks. Cotton's natural fibers will soak up and retain moisture, and your feet will become a perfect breeding ground for painful blisters and coldness. Wool and synthetic blend socks offer great insulation and wick moisture away from skin, helping to keep your feet dry and comfortable.

★ **DRESS APPROPRIATELY.** Proper clothing will help keep you comfortable and healthy on the trail. *Flashy*, *Expensive*, and *Gadget-y* don't mean a blinkin' thing if they can't support a great hiking experience. Really, after a good hike, nobody looks like they've just stepped out of a fashion magazine.

Prevent Hypothermia

Hypothermia occurs when a person's core body temperature becomes abnormally low. This extremely dangerous condition is also marked by the rapid deterioration and ultimate failure of mental and physical functions. Because a body loses heat more quickly when it is wet, staying warm and dry is essential.

Know that the weather often changes without warning in Yellowstone. Snow and sleet may fall at any time of year, and rain and wind are not uncommon. A hot 80°F (27°C) summer day can easily become a cold 20°F (-7°C) summer night. Pack a hat and gloves no matter when you visit the park. Being prepared with the proper clothing can help ward off hypothermia.

★ **ACT BEFORE THE FACT**. Before you get wet, put on your rain gear. Before you get cold, put on your warm gear. Don't wait until it's too late to use your stuff!

Uncontrollable shivering, impaired motor function, slurred speech, memory lapses, jumbled speech, and exhaustion are all signs of hypothermia. For mild cases, bundle the body into warm, dry clothes and feed warm liquids. For severe cases, immediately seek help.

Take a Trail Kit

A trail kit is a compilation of everything you should need and could need on the trail. If you find yourself in a jam on your hike, you need to be able to depend primarily on yourself and your gear to get you back on track. Self-sufficiency is a must.

Included below is a Trail Kit Checklist. Read through it, determine which items you may need for your hike, and pack your kit accordingly. If you're taking a quarter-mile boardwalk stroll, you may not need a bunch of snacks and an emergency whistle, but if you're embarking on a backcountry trek, it'd be wise to bring these things along.

Trail Kit Checklist

___ **Backpack / Day Pack**

Your backpack or day pack contains items from your trail kit, extra clothing, gear, and everything else that will accompany you on your hike. Stash the items you need to access quickly in your pack's outside pockets. When packing your backpack, keep its center of gravity as high as possible to prevent it from dragging you back.

___ **Compass / GPS**

If you bring a compass, know how to use it before you embark on your hike. Nobody wants to desperately try to remember the ten minutes of orienteering instruction from your sixth-grade outdoor education field trip. Your panicked memory may not be reliable enough to keep you on the right path.

The popularity of geocaching and interactive treasure hunts can make a GPS a fun tool to take along on your hike, so be sure it has an adequate charge before you stash it in your backpack. Note that the hike descriptions in this Fat Ass Guide include trailhead coordinates for easy location.

___ Maps

Bring a topographical map if you're heading into backcountry areas. Everyone in your hiking group should study the map beforehand and become familiar with the adventure territory. Keep your map dry by securing it in a watertight bag in your pack.

___ Flashlight

Your flashlight should be small and waterproof. You don't need a big searchlight beacon, just something that will adequately guide you through the darkness if you need it. A headlamp or head-mounted flashlight is a good hands-free idea. Make sure your flashlight has working batteries. Hand-crank battery-free flashlights are also a popular alternative to battery-sucking torches.

___ Water and Water Bottle

Humans need to hydrate to function. Yellowstone is a very dry place. Good news! Cheap ol' water is a most refreshing beverage for the job. Bring a container large enough to hold more than the amount of water you expect to need on the hike - at least 32 ounces for every hour on the trail.

Fill up your water bottle from a domestic source before you arrive at the trailhead. Don't count on developed trailheads to supply potable (drinkable) water. If the trailhead has a nearby source of potable water, don't be afraid of filling up your water bottle. The pump might be creaky, and the water might look interesting, but just let it settle for a moment, and chances are you'll be a-ok. Add electrolyte powder for a palatable treat. Electrolyte powder helps replenish necessary salts lost through sweating. Be sure to drink even if you don't feel thirsty.

Leave soft drinks, caffeinated beverages, and alcoholic libations at home because they leach fluid from your system and actively work to dehydrate you.

★ **KNOW YOUR H2O**. Unless you have serious water purification tablets or a water treatment device and know what you're doing, don't drink water out of streams, rivers, lakes, or other waterbodies because you may also ingest dangerous bacteria, parasites, and other creepy waterborne contaminates like Giardia, which will leave you with zero appetite, abdominal cramping, and diarrhea. If you suspect you've been infected with Giardiasis, consult a doctor.

___ Snacks

As you hike, you burn calories. You need food to fuel your mainframe, or else it'll eventually start to burn muscle, and that will zap your energy. Granola bars, jerky, dried fruit, and trail mix are all energy-pumping munchies that'll keep you going on the trail. Leave the gummy bears and cheese puffs at home. They have little nutritional value, convert into very little energy, and will make you feel crappy.

If you are hiking in bear country, pack your snacks in double zip bags or airtight containers. Do not bring along any savory meats, fish, or fats. A tuna sub buried in your backpack will just make you smell like a walking deli to a bear.

___ Matches - Fire Starter

Packing waterproof matches or a fire starter in your trail kit is an excellent idea if you're heading into the backcountry, even if you aren't expecting an overnight trek. Remember, you are fortifying yourself against a worst-case scenario. If the evolution of the human species has taught us anything, the ability to control fire is one of the defining accomplishments of humankind. Opt for waterproof matches, which have waxed heads to keep them dry. Flint and steel is a purist alternative to traditional matches while cotton swabbed in kerosene, paraffin blocks, and fire sticks are also handy tools for creating quick blazes.

___ Knife

A knife is a survival must-have which can help you construct a shelter, get food, prepare meals, make a fire, and cut bandages, among other handy things. The ability to adequately accomplish survival tasks with the proper tools will help keep you calm and in control in an emergency. A good knife is stronger than anything you can assemble in the field and will save a lot of wear and tear on bare hands trying to reach the same objectives. Keep your knife sharp and handle it with respect.

___ First Aid Kit

Bring a first aid kit, and make sure that every person in your group knows how to use it. A first aid kit will treat both minor injuries and stabilize more serious injuries until additional help arrives. Your first aid kit should include a small pair of blunt-nosed scissors, adhesive bandages for blisters and small cuts, gauze for securing wounds, triangular bandages for slings, antiseptic to clean wounds, foot treatments like corn pads, and pain killers. Be sure to bring along any medication that you may need. Don't forget the epinephrine auto-injector to ward of anaphylactic shock if you are allergic to insect bites!

___ Insect Repellant

Insect repellant will prove a godsend in Yellowstone's many moist insect-loving areas. The most effective insect repellants contain DEET used in at least a 20% solution. Spray both your clothes and exposed skin in accordance with product directions for maximum benefit. Special permethrin-treated clothing also helps ward off disease-carrying biters. Avoid attracters like scented lotions and bedazzled accessories.

___ Bear Pepper Spray

Invest in bear pepper spray and know how to use it. Bear pepper spray is a non-lethal aerosol spray that is used as a disabling weapon against bears. When a bear inhales the spray, it causes irritation to its eyes and skin; induces coughing, choking and nausea; and temporarily impedes the bear's ability to breathe. If you are unfortunate enough to encounter an aggressive bear, bear pepper spray may save both your life and the life of the bear.

Use bear pepper spray, NOT personal defense pepper spray or law enforcement pepper spray. Make sure your bear pepper spray contains "Capsaicin or related Capsaicinoids" or is "derived from Oleoresin of Capsicum" with an active ingredient of between 1% and 2%. The canister should be at least 7.9 ounces. Federal regulations require that the bear pepper spray be marked as "bear deterrent" or "to deter bears from attacking humans."

Everyone in your hiking group should have their own bear pepper spray. Consider that you may encounter and engage more than one bear on your hike. Make sure the bear pepper spray is accessible at all times on your hike and is not buried in your backpack.

★ **BEAR PEPPER SPRAY IS FOR BEARS ONLY!** Do not spray bear pepper spray on your clothes, your gear, or any other person. If you come into contact with bear spay, flush the contact area with plenty of water.

(See **Wildlife Safety - Bears** for more information.)

___ Noisemaker - Whistle

Many hikers opt to proactively avoid interactions with animals by attaching a rattling noisemaker to their packs. Understand that a noisemaker is only one tool to help scare away wildlife and is in no way a substitute for awareness, good judgment, and being armed with more powerful deterrents like bear pepper spray.

A whistle is useful in identifying your location in case of an emergency because it is louder and takes less energy to operate than yelling and screaming.

___ Hat and Gloves - Sunglasses - Sunscreen

Major body heat is lost through the head, so keep that noggin protected! Yellowstone is known for quick-whipping storms and extended snowfall, so pack a hat and gloves, even in early summer. A brimmed hat and sunglasses will help keep your eyes shaded and protected from UV rays. Sunscreen is an absolute must, even on cloudy days. Yellowstone's high altitude makes exposure to sun and its harmful elements especially potent.

___ Rain Gear

Fast-developing storms frequently roll through Yellowstone with sunny skies quickly filling with rain clouds. A rain jacket or poncho will help keep you dry and comfortable on your adventure, and may even prevent dangerous hypothermia. Most rain gear is lightweight and compact, so be sure to include it in your kit!

___ Walking Stick - Hiking Poles

Some people find walking sticks and hiking poles very useful on trails with inclines, declines, and bumpy terrain because they can boost balance, increase endurance, and reduce knee stress by distributing some of the workload from the legs to the arms. Some people find walking sticks and hiking poles annoying and cumbersome. If you're not sure which category you fall into, try them out before your hike. Make sure you are using them properly by checking your technique with a knowledgeable outfitter to adequately measure their worth and reap their benefits.

___ Binoculars - Camera - Notepad

Binoculars, a camera, and a notepad may enhance your hiking experience. Binoculars are useful in viewing wildlife from afar, and can help animal watchers keep a safe distance while appreciating free-roaming beasts. A camera and a notepad can conveniently capture awesome adventure memories and record hiking observations.

___ Cell Phone - Identification

Carrying important identifying information will help streamline any worst-case-scenario rescue and recovery efforts. A cell phone may be helpful in reaching out for help during an emergency situation, but understand that many areas of Yellowstone are too remote to accommodate cell phone service. Bring your cell phone but don't depend on it!

Post It

If you choose to hike alone, tell a trusted friend where you're going and when you expect to return. Many Yellowstone trails, especially backcountry trails, have trail registers at the trailhead. Always sign in and out at the register. Trail registers help park officials know which trails are in use and where to look if questions arise about a hiker's whereabouts.

Safety

IN CASE OF EMERGENCY DIAL 911.

Personal Safety

Remoteness of national parks combined with throngs of temporary visitors sadly creates an environment attractive to lawbreakers looking to sneak around and operate unnoticed. Don't assume that federal budgets adequately allow for comprehensive staffing of rangers and support of law enforcement personnel within national parks.

Think smart. When parking your vehicle at a trailhead, lock it and take your valuables with you. Do not leave anything in your vehicle that might tempt thieves. Unfortunately, criminal minds understand that many hikers both trust goodwill among fellow wilderness enjoyers and believe that areas within national parks offer unbreachable levels of security. Hooligans exploit the optimism and positivity of the human condition; as a result, many vehicles have been burglarized in broad daylight at trailheads, visitor's centers, and points of interest.

With any circumstance, listen your instincts, trust your judgment, and don't become disoriented by the magic of newness. As a society we want to connect with our fellow man and share experiences, and we often seek out ways to forge bonds with others. Awesome adventures brim with opportunities to reach out, make new friends, and welcome strangers into our lives. This is not to say we should shut ourselves off and limit our horizons, but rather proceed with eyes wide open.

DANGEROUSLY TRUE:

COFFEE AND KILLERS

"A cup of coffee, please." The barista frowns and eyes the man who had just ignored a long line of waiting customers and approached the counter of her Mammoth Hot Springs coffee stand. "I'm sorry," the barista says, pointing to the line, "but

you'll have to wait your turn." The man nods and takes his place in the back of the line. The line moves quickly and soon the man is standing before her again. She hands him his coffee and he thanks her, mentioning that he is a film producer on his way to California. The barista smiles; she is an actress. "Maybe I can put you in a movie some time," the man says and leaves her a nice-sized tip. He disappears through the door and into Yellowstone's great wilds.

A few days later, the café supervisor hands the barista a flyer. A familiar face stares back at her, framed in a wanted poster from the FBI. "He was in here the other day," the barista says, "good tipper, but strange."

The man who patronized my friend's coffee stand was an escaped convict who had broken out of a prison in Arizona where he had been serving time for murder. On the run with a fellow escapee, he committed a double homicide of a 60-year-old couple in New Mexico before heading to Yellowstone. The convicts were eventually captured.

Firearms

For slingers looking to flash a little gun, persons legally possessing firearms may do so in Yellowstone National Park provided that all federal, state, and local laws are followed. This federal law went into effect on February 22, 2010.

Because Yellowstone includes portions of Wyoming, Montana, and Idaho, gun carriers must comply with applicable (and sometimes differing) state laws. Verify laws and compliance requirements before entering the park! Understand that some Yellowstone facilities prohibit gun toting. Know that there is very little that you can do with your gun in Yellowstone, so do not even consider it an adequate safeguard against dangerous wildlife! (See **Wildlife Safety** for more information.)

Geothermal Features

Yellowstone and its more than 10,000 hydrothermal features account for about half of the planet's naturally heated water systems and provide an unmatched opportunity to experience some of the world's most awesome hot water gems. Powerful turrets of water gushing out of the park's famous geysers may mask the inherent fragility of geothermal features, their delicate plumbing chambers, and the unique microorganism colonies that thrive in their waters. Use hot water safety practices at all times in the park!

Don't hike at night in hydrothermal areas, stay on boardwalks and walkways, and watch your step when venturing off-trail in other areas. Thin crusts may hide deadly scalding water. Understand that constantly changing geothermal landscapes may disguise hot water dangers; in fact, even native wildlife is not immune to thermal hazards. If you enter an area that smells like boiled meat, a buffalo may have very well taken a tumble into a nearby hot spring.

Do not throw objects, natural or otherwise, into hydrothermal features. Objects can block vents, change activity, and destroy once-active features. Be aware that hydrogen sulfide, carbon dioxide, and carbon monoxide may be present in hydrothermal areas. If you feel nauseous, lightheaded, or sick, get the heck out of the area.

Do not eat, drink, or smoke in Yellowstone's hydrothermal areas. Cigarette butts have a habit of magically multiplying and ultimately end up choking thermal vents and destroying hydrothermal activity. Some gasses and deposits swirling about thermal areas are flammable. Sparking butts could cause explosions and fires, as well as create deadly fumes.

Don't inhale thermal steam. Many thermal waters contain organisms that may cause fatal skin rashes, infections, meningitis, and Legionnaire's Disease. If you decide to go for a dip in park-approved thermal runoff waterways like the Boiling River, don't dunk your head underwater. Swimming or entering water that is entirely thermally produced is prohibited.

Lakes, Rivers, and Waterways

Yellowstone's waterbodies are dang cold! Yellowstone Lake, Lewis Lake, and Shoshone Lake are late breakers, often ice-covered until early June. Their temperatures, rarely topping 50°F (10°C), are heart-stopping cold! Use extreme caution around these lakes. You have only minutes to escape too-cold water before your muscles spasm, render safe swimming impossible, and seal a grim fate.

Understand that Yellowstone's creeks, streams, and rivers may be massive, fast-flowing, cold, and dangerous to cross. Spring and early summer snowmelt makes many waterways impossible to cross until at least July. Rain may also quickly amplify water levels and intensity of flow. If your hike requires a fording, check at the ranger station nearest to the trailhead before your adventure for information on current conditions.

★ **A SAFE FORD**. When fording a creek, stream, or river, search along the banks for the safest crossing, which may not be exactly where the river meets the trail. Keep your shoes on your feet as bare feet may slip on slick rocks or get cut on sharp, hidden obstacles. Make sure your pack is loose, unclipped around your body, and easily ditch-able in case you take a tumble into the water. Use a stabilizer like a stick or hiking pole, and focus your eyes on a distant point to help balance during the fording. If applicable, cross as a group, holding hands and making a chain.

Altitude

Most of Yellowstone National Park sits above 7,500 feet (2,286 m). At elevated altitudes, some people may experience the effects of lower pressure and less oxygen-rich air. A slight burning in lungs grappling for oxygen is common. Take relaxed breaths to offset the discomfort. If you are not used to high-elevation environments, allow your body time to adjust. Don't take that high mountain climb right off the bat. Allow a night for acclimatization, and the next day ease into hiking with one of Yellowstone's lower elevation trails. Remember to take your time, travel at a steady pace, stay hydrated, and don't overdo it.

Note that higher elevations often do not support shade-providing trees. These exposed areas offer plenty of opportunity for sunburn even if the day feels nice and cool. Wear a hat and slather on the sunscreen! Persons with respiratory issues should be especially diligent in high altitude areas. Choose your physical activity wisely.

Storms

Weather in Yellowstone is unpredictable, and some high-elevation areas remain covered with snow throughout the year. Strong storms may blow through the park at any time, rapidly dropping temperatures. Make sure you are armed with warm clothing, including a hat, gloves, and rain gear, no matter the forecast.

Practice storm safety by immediately taking cover and staying out of exposed areas like ridges, shores, open meadows, singularly standing trees, and lone boulders during lightning storms. Don't pull a Ben Franklin! Distance yourself from electricity-attracting metal objects. If you are hiking in a group, spread out to avoid getting chain-zapped.

Be prepared for gusty afternoons that may topple trees. Expect summertime daytime highs to reach into the 80s, and nighttime lows to dip into the 30s, at low elevations. Remember to always check weather conditions before you hike!

Fire

Personal fires should be created, maintained, and extinguished with great care in accordance with park regulations. Check at any ranger station for information about what areas in Yellowstone support campfires and backpacking stoves. Usually, open wood fires are only allowed in fire rings at specific campsites and at specific times of year. Practice fire safety: Keep it small, keep your eye on it at all times, and make sure it is dead cold before you leave!

Wildfires should be actively avoided. Never attempt to put out a wildfire! If you do so, you will be posing a grave risk to yourself and will be interfering with a significant natural cycle. If you spot a fire in progress, leave the area and immediately notify a ranger. Yellowstone has a very detailed and very specific wildfire management plan that in many circumstances allows wildfires to naturally burn.

Wildfire is an important rejuvenating element for Yellowstone's ecosystem and actually increases wildlife habitat diversity. Post-fire soil is extremely fertile, and dead trees provide excellent homes for birds and small animals. The survival of some vegetation, like the lodgepole pine, is dependent on wildfire, as particular seedpods only open in extreme heat.

Insects

Mosquitoes and ticks are the two biggest bug threats in Yellowstone. Mosquitoes thrive in wet areas with comfortable temperatures and swarm near Yellowstone's lakes, rivers, and swamps in May through August. Apply repellant containing DEET in at least a 20% solution, and wear permethrin-treated clothing to avoid itchy bites.

Small parasitic, blood-thirsty ticks love Yellowstone's grassy meadows. Predominantly active in mid-spring through mid-summer, ticks may carry debilitating Rocky Mountain spotted fever and Lyme disease. Actively avoid tick contact with insect repellant and by keeping your clothes tucked to your core. Ticks are shifty, so always check for hangers-on after your hike. If you catch a tick on your body, use tweezers to gently pull it out as close to the burrowing head as possible. If you fail to pull the entire tick out or notice any flu-like symptoms, facial paralysis, or skin spots, seek immediate medical attention.

Berries, Nuts, Mushrooms, and Plants

You can pick 'em to eat 'em but be absolutely certain that what you're shoveling into your mouth is edible. Don't assume that because something looks delicious and juicy that it's safe to eat, or that because something looks like a raspberry that it is a raspberry. Many poisonous plants bear striking resemblances to their harmless counterparts. Don't take risks in sampling wild, unfamiliar foods. You must be

100% sure that what you intend to eat is safe to eat. This will help prevent fatal poisoning.

Stop the spread of invasive and noxious vegetation by cleaning any weeds or seeds from your clothing and gear before visiting Yellowstone. Don't go digging around in the park's soil, move plants from one place to another, or take any flower or plant home. Not only is it illegal, but you could also be damaging an ecosystem for many lifetimes.

Wildlife Safety

Yellowstone is teeming with all sorts of spectacular wildlife; in fact, Yellowstone has the greatest concentration of mammals in the continental United States. Simply look around to see many of the 200 animal species that live in the park, including buffalo, bears, wolves, coyotes, foxes, moose, pronghorn, bighorn sheep, mountain goats, deer, bobcats, cougars, badgers, otters, beavers, pikas, hares, porcupines, eagles, herons, falcons, owls, turkeys, and pelicans, to name a few... phew.

Although these magnificent creatures may look majestic and adorable on greeting cards, do not forget that wild animals are inherently dangerous. An animal's seemingly peaceful nature may belie a threatened beast about to lash out at any moment in unexpected and deadly ways. A biting, kicking, goring animal is no fun, especially if you're on the receiving end. Know that breeding seasons make animals especially temperamental. Every year Yellowstone visitors are injured by animals.

Thankfully, nearly all animal - human conflict is avoidable, so do not approach, feed, crowd, follow, or harass wildlife: big game, small game, or otherwise. Take special care to avoid females with their young. As fun as it is, do not mimic animal sounds, including wolf howls. Do not use tools such as animal calls to attract or disrupt wildlife.

To reiterate, do not under any circumstance feed wildlife. Animals that develop a taste for human food often lose their fear of civilization. Because the animals return to areas where food is easily accessible, they are difficult to relocate.

Wildlife management teams often have to euthanize these animals. Wolves were killed in 2009 and 2011 because they repeatedly sought food from visitors.

★ **THEY DID WHAT, NOW?** Don't, for the love of all that's sacred, hoist your kid up on a buffalo's back to take a picture. Don't entice your girlfriend to put her arm around a buffalo so that you can take her picture while you seek safety behind your car. Two separate scenarios, both eye-witnessed. To quote a Yellowstone security guard friend, "Sure I'll explain the rules to visitors, but there's no way I'm wrestling a buffalo to protect a stupid family."

IF YOU SEE A PERSON DOING SOMETHING THAT ENDANGERS EITHER PARK USERS OR WILDLIFE, IMMEDIATELY REPORT IT TO A PARK RANGER.

Bears

Make sure everyone in your hiking group is informed about bear safety. Both grizzly bears and black bears roam the forests and meadows of Yellowstone's vast bear country. Although bears are not naturally ferocious, they can be extremely dangerous when engaged. Be vigilant, actively avoid bears, detour as needed, and carry easily accessible bear pepper spray. *You must stay at least 100 yards (91 m) away from bears.*

Bears most commonly engage humans because they are either surprised, protecting their young, or safeguarding a food source. Hiking in gullies, in forests, and along waterways masks scents and increases chances of stumbling upon a bear. Limit the propensity for bear encounters by hiking in groups of three or more people. Bears have excellent senses of smell, so do not tote around any savory meats, fats, or fragrant toiletries on your hike. Keep snacks and food in double zip bags or airtight containers.

Hike during the day to avoid prime dusk, dawn, and nighttime bear hours. Make noise by loudly talking, singing, clapping, or rattling a noisemaker. Watch for bear tracks, droppings, and evidence of digging and clawing. If you see any of these signs, discontinue your hike. If you see a cub, immediately leave the area. Stay away from dead animals, carcasses, and anything that smells like rotting meat as it could be under the protection of a nearby bear. Inform rangers of any dead animals near trails.

If you see a bear from an ample distance and the bear doesn't see you, detour a wide breadth behind and downwind of the bear. Do not interfere with the bear's path.

If you see a bear at close range, do not make any sudden movements. Your sprint could make you look like juicy prey. Despite a bear's lumbering stature, it can run super fast, up to 40 mph (64 km/h). Bears can also swim and climb trees. Stay calm, stay still, avoid direct and challenging eye contact, and talk calmly to the bear. Hopefully it will go away. Teeth gnashing, panting, growling, staring, and stamping feet are all warning signs from bears that they want you to back down. If a bear charges at you, stand your ground. Do not run. Bears often bluff charge, veering away or stopping at the last moment.

If an aggressive bear gets within 20 to 30 feet (6 to 9 m) of you, deploy your bear pepper spray. Aim for the bear's eyes and snout in a clear path. If you discharge bear pepper spray, leave the area immediately because bears sometimes like to return for a good sniff. Discharge bear pepper spray only if a bear is behaving aggressively and only as a last course of action.

If a bear makes physical contact with you, drop to the ground and play dead. Keep your pack on because you will need it to protect your body. Clasp your hands over the back of your neck, lie face down on your stomach with your legs extended, and stay silent to diffuse your perceived threat to the bear. This position will also hamper the bear's ability to flip you over. Remain still until a few minutes after the bear has left the area to ensure its complete departure.

If you feel that a bear views you as prey and is following you, be aggressive! Shout, make a lot of noise, look as big as possible, use bear pepper spray, and do everything you can to look like you are not an easy target. Luckily, this is an extremely rare scenario.

DANGEROUSLY TRUE:

TERROR ON WAPITI LAKE TRAIL

July 6, 2011. A husband and wife from California take a morning hike down Wapiti Lake Trail, near the South Rim of the Grand Canyon of the Yellowstone River. A fellow hiker points out a mother grizzly bear with her cubs in a nearby meadow, approximately 500 yards (457 m) away from the trail. The couple photographs the bear and continues their hike.

On the return trek, the husband and wife notice that the bear and her cubs are now on the trail, 100 yards (91 m) away from them. They immediately turn around and retreat in the opposite direction. The bear begins to follow them, much to their unease. As the bear continues its approach, the husband yells, "Run!" and he and his wife sprint down the trail.

The wife jumps behind a fallen tree and watches from her hiding place as the bear mauls her screaming husband. The mother bear knocks him in the head and bites his knee, ripping open his femoral artery. The bear returns for the wife, picking her up by her backpack and dropping her on the ground. She remains still. The bear eventually leaves the area.

The wife moves over to her husband and desperately tries to call 911 on her phone, but she is unable to get a signal in the backcountry. A nearby hiker, hearing the screams from the trail, is able to reach emergency services. It's too late. The husband dies on the scene from blunt force trauma and blood loss. It is the first fatal grizzly mauling at Yellowstone in 25 years.

In this Dangerously True scenario, investigators conclude that when the husband and wife ran from the bear, the motion may have induced the bear to chase and attack them. Investigators further determine that because the bear acted in a defensive manner to protect its cubs and did not have any known prior contact with humans, it would be allowed to roam free. Subsequent DNA and footprint samples demonstrate that the bear was involved in another deadly mauling in the park a few weeks later. (See **DANGEROUSLY TRUE: MARY MOUNTAIN MAULING**.) The bear is euthanized, and the cubs are sent to the West Yellowstone

Grizzly and Wolf Discovery Center's refuge for orphaned and injured wildlife. Every year an average of one visitor sustains a bear-related injury in the park.

★ **AMERICANUS OR HORRIBILIS?** Yellowstone hosts both grizzly bears (Ursus arctos horribilis) and black bears (Ursus americanus) in a variety of colorings. The two bears are most visually distinguishable by their physical characteristics.

Grizzly bears are larger than black bears and can weigh over 700 pounds (318 kg). Grizzly bears have a shoulder hump, and their butts are lower than their shoulders. They are most often spotted in the Lamar Valley and in the Hayden Valley north of Yellowstone Lake.

Black bears can weigh over 300 pounds (136 kg). They do not have a shoulder hump, and their butts are taller than their heads. Black bears also have rounder ears than grizzly bears. Black bears are most often spotted in the Canyon - Tower area and in the Madison - Old Faithful area. Grizzly bears and black bears are most active in the late spring and in the fall, as they gorge themselves for hibernation.

Grizzly Bear © Rusty Dodson - Dreamstime.com

Black Bear © Chrisimages - Dreamstime.com

Buffalo (Bison)

So awesome. So majestic. So American. Bison (the scientific name for buffalo) are the largest land mammals in North America. Between 3,000 and 4,000 of the big beasts live in Yellowstone; in fact, Yellowstone National Park is the only place in the United States where bison have romped in the wild since prehistoric times.

You're bound to participate in at least one buffalo jam (a traffic jam caused by buffalo) in your time at the park, so you'd better get wise to the facts. Males weigh up to 2,000 pounds (907 kg) and females weigh up to 1,000 pounds (454 kg). Don't let that heft fool you! Buffalo are fast, with running speeds of over 30 mph (48 km/h). Although they seem relaxed standing along highways and hanging out in meadows, they can be extremely dangerous, very aggressive, and can gore you in a jiffy. Every year visitors are seriously injured by buffalo. *You must stay at least 25 yards (23 m) away from buffalo!*

Buffalo (Bison) © Tony Campbell - Dreamstime.com

Wolves and Coyotes

Wolves are native to Yellowstone, freely roaming the park until 1926 when a society freaked out over predation killed the last wolf pack. In 1995, 14 gray wolves from Alberta, Canada were reintroduced into Yellowstone. As of January 2011, approximately 120 wolves live within the boundaries of the park. Gray wolves can be gray, black, or white and weigh 80 to 100 pounds (36 to 45 kg). They roam forests and meadows and mainly eat elk and deer. Pack territories include most of Yellowstone, with the exception of the south central area of the park. *You must stay at least 100 yards (91 m) away from wolves!*

Coyotes are more common and much smaller than wolves. Adult coyotes weigh between 25 and 35 pounds (11 to 16 kg). They hang out in forests, meadows, and grasslands, and mainly eat rodents, small animals, carrion, and occasionally baby elk. You may see coyotes begging for food on the side of the road. Don't feed them! *You must stay at least 25 yards (23 m) away from coyotes!*

Gray Wolf © Steven Davis - Dreamstime.com

Coyote © Alptraum - Dreamstime.com

Other Exciting Game

Elk (wapiti) are incredibly abundant in Yellowstone, with one of the largest wild herds in North America thriving in the park's Northern Range. Summer elk populations can reach 20,000 strong, and the hoofed creatures are most often found in forests and meadows. Males (bulls) weigh approximately 700 pounds (318 kg), and females (cows) weigh about 500 pounds (227 kg).

Elk © Tony Campbell - Dreamstime.com

Moose are on the loose around Yellowstone's wet areas like marshes, rivers, and lakes. Less than 200 moose live in the park. Massive members of the deer family, males (bulls) weigh up to 1,000 pounds (454 kg), and females (cows) weigh up to 900 pounds (408 kg). They mainly eat aquatic plants, willows, and berries.

Mule deer make up most of the deer population in Yellowstone, with summer numbers reaching 2,500 and winter numbers registering significantly less. Mule deer romp in forests and grassy areas. Males (bucks) weigh up to 250 pounds (113 kg), and females (does) weigh up to 175 pounds

(79 kg).

Bighorn sheep are found on Yellowstone's mountainsides, canyons, and cliffs. Park populations number 275 of the wooly beasts. Males (rams) weigh up to 300 pounds (136 kg), and females (ewes) weigh up to 200 pounds (91 kg). Horns - found on both males and females - can weigh nearly 40 pounds (18 kg)!

Bighorn Sheep © Rinus Baak - Dreamstime.com

You must stay at least 25 yards (23 m) away from elk, moose, deer, and bighorn sheep!

★ **REPORT IT**. If an animal attacks or injures you or someone in your party, immediately notify the proper authorities even if you've done something stupid to provoke the animal. This will help protect other park visitors from bearing similar consequences.

Hike It Right

It's easy to think that we can just traipse into the natural world and do whatever the heck we want because the powerful forces of Mother Nature are mighty equalizers. In reality, what we do matters a great deal because ecosystems are fragile and susceptible to warped changes by even the smallest of human interferences. Because most of you using this Fat Ass Guide won't be venturing too far off the beaten path into Yellowstone's solitary backcountry, having the skills to successfully interact with your fellow hikers is tops. Good Practices Guidelines outlines important hiking strategy musts. Hike It Right also highlights specific Yellowstone trail characteristics and regulations.

Trail Markings

There are trails practically everywhere in Yellowstone, be it modern manmade paths, wild animal trails, supply routes, historic paths, or old stagecoach roads. Trails in Yellowstone that are surveyed, mapped, and occasionally monitored by park officials are marked with orange flags on trees and posts at trailheads and access points. These trails are usually maintained, but some less-trodden paths can be difficult to find. Yellowstone's constantly changing landscape, particularly from wildfire and hydrothermal activity, may make trail-finding challenging. Many trail intersections have signposts that include distance and directional information, but again this is not always the case. Know your route before you begin your hike.

Pets Prohibited

Yellowstone's many hydrothermal features are dangerous to pets. Dogs in particular have trouble distinguishing water temperatures; as a result, many have died jumping into super hot water in the park - and some of their owners have died trying to save them. Pets also have uncanny abilities to call attention to other animals and tussle with wildlife, which often ruins the nature experience for other trail users.

Wayward pets can end up as tasty treats for Yellowstone's carnivorous beasts. Additionally, the interaction of animals from different habitats can increase the spread of certain communicable diseases. For these reasons, PETS ARE NOT PERMITTED ON TRAILS IN YELLOWSTONE NATIONAL PARK. In all other areas of the park, pets must be leashed.

Good Practices Guidelines

Following these guidelines will help keep your fat ass out of trouble and keep the good times rolling.

- **Stretch**

Avoid hiking injuries by gently stretching before and after your hike. Stretching helps warm up muscles and increases flexibility, so your body doesn't freak out, get out of whack, and sustain injury on the trail. Remove your backpack, relax, and carefully stretch your neck, arms, waist, and lower back; then, focus on your legs, hamstrings, and calves. Each stretch should last for about 30 seconds. Don't over do it! You should not feel pain during your pre-hike warm-up.

- **Sign In and Out**

Sign in and out at any trailhead with a register. Trail registers help park officials recognize which trails are in use and where to look for absent adventurers.

- **Obey Trailhead Rules**

Many trailheads post trail-specific rules. Trailheads may also post valuable updates on trail conditions, environmental concerns, wildlife activity, and special programs. Read, know, and follow the postings and updates to ensure that you get the most out of your hiking adventure.

- **Observe Trail Etiquette**

Share the trail, and understand that some trails accommodate multiple modes of transportation. Yield to horseback riders, and watch out for bicyclists. Stay to the right on the trail except to pass. When passing, give a clear notice. If you are hiking in a group, don't hog the path. If you need to take a break or a picture, move off the trail so that it's clear for others. Be friendly to your fellow hikers, and don't pollute the airspace with unnecessary loudness or hooliganism.

- **Stay on the Trail**

Don't cut switchbacks or take shortcuts. There's a reason why a trail is placed in a particular location. Sometimes it may be to bypass a dangerous geographical feature, a wildlife habitat, or an area sensitive to contact. If you venture off the trail, you risk getting lost. Read all available trail markings. Don't just follow a group of hikers heading in a particular direction and trust that they're going where you want to go.

- **Keep Your Eye on the Kids**

If you are hiking with children, keep them in your direct line of sight at all times, even in familiar areas. Don't let your child run out of your reach. The impulsivity of children can make it difficult for them to obey trail rules, and they can cause serious damage to themselves, others, and the environment. Nobody wants their child wandering ahead, ending up lost, getting mauled by a wild animal, falling into an off-trail crevasse, tripping into a boiling spring, or plummeting to their death.

- **Do Not Disturb, Disrupt, or Feed Wildlife**

Yield to that bear on the trail. Yellowstone is its home, and its job is not to be the star of your "look how awesome my vacation was, oh crap, now it's coming for me" video. You risk serious injury and even death to both yourself and the animal by interacting with it. Do not feed wildlife, begging or otherwise. Do not mimic animal sounds. Review **Wildlife Safety** for more information. *You must stay 100 yards (91 m) away from bears and wolves and 25 yards (23 m) away from all other wildlife!*

- **Leave Only Footprints**

Pack out your trash. Yellowstone banned its own open garbage dumps in 1970. Don't bury your junk or drop it in pit toilets. Take trash disposal seriously: It's an important wildlife management tool. Stray garbage attracts animals to people places, posing risks to both wildlife and park visitors.

Don't murky up Yellowstone's lovely waters with foreign materials like soap, waste, cigarettes, or food. Minimum and low-impact hiking helps keep Yellowstone pristine.

• Take Only Pictures

Preserve the memory of your hike with a photograph, not a wild souvenir. Leave bark, rocks, sticks, flowers, antlers, animal parts, live animals, feathers, seeds, bones, any natural elements, and any artifacts where you find them! Don't go digging around for treasures, and don't destroy or deface anything that you may come across. If you stumble upon something significant, leave it where you find it, and report it to a ranger. Stay on the right side of the law and leave them things alone!

• Answering Nature's Call

If available, use trailhead restrooms. If you are on the trail and the urge to relieve yourself overtakes you, find a spot that is at least 100 feet (31 m) away from any trail, water source, or campsite to do your business. Urinating near the trail may unsafely attract wildlife to your salt deposits and lure wild creatures too close to humans. Bury solid human waste in holes at least eight inches deep. Pack out your toilet paper and other hygiene products.

Know Before You Go

As a final review before you begin your hiking adventure, make sure you absolutely know:

- The current weather forecast
- The trail, the terrain, and their current conditions
- Proper clothing and equipment
- Good hiking practices
- Trail rules and regulations
- Wildlife safety
- Environmental safety
- Hypothermia prevention
- Emergency protocol

Terminology

Hiking Terms

Backcountry - a remote wilderness area

Logjam - logs blocking a river

Loop hike - a hike circling on a continuous path back to the trailhead

Out-and-back hike - a hike to a specific destination where the return trek backtracks down the same trail to the trailhead

Shuttle hike - a hike where the end point differs from the starting point, requiring a shuttle (like a car or a bicycle) to connect the two access points

Spur trail - a path that branches off the main trail

Yellowstone Terms

Bobbysox Trees - trees ringed by smothering mineral deposits in hydrothermal areas

Caldera - a large volcanic crater

Fumarole - (steam vent) an opening by or in a volcano where hot gasses escape

Geothermal - relating to heat produced by the earth

Geyser - a hot spring with compressed subterranean plumbing where water boils and which often shoots out water and steam

Geyser basin - a distinguishable region containing a group of hydrothermal features like geysers, mudpots, fumaroles, and hot springs

Geyserite - opaline silica deposited by hot springs and geysers

Hot spring - a body of hot water, usually heated by underground volcanic activity, which does not have a compressed subterranean system

Hydrothermal - relating to water heated inside the earth's crust

Mudpot - a hydrothermal feature where microorganisms convert thermal gas to sulfuric acid, breaking down rock into clay

Obsidian - dark, glassy volcanic rock created when lava quickly solidified without crystallizing

Rhyolite - fine-grained volcanic rock

Sinter - hard siliceous or calcareous material deposited by mineral springs

Thermophile - a microorganism that thrives in hot temperatures

Travertine - calcareous rock deposited by mineral springs as water dissolves limestone (calcium carbonate)

Yellowstone National Park

Yellowstone National Park is the first officially designated national park in the United States, earning that distinction on March 1, 1872. Sprawling 3,472 square miles (8,992 square km), or 2.2 million acres (890,308 hectares), through Wyoming and into Montana and Idaho, it's an extraordinary place of history, scenery, wildlife, and geology - a perfect place to explore on foot!

Map of Yellowstone National Park

The map above depicts Yellowstone's trails, by number. Each number precedes the corresponding trail name and description found under the appropriate region heading. Stars denote major park villages. Trail 1, just north of Mammoth Hot Springs Village, is **1. Boiling River**, found under the expanded Mammoth Hot Springs and North Entrance Area region heading, which you'll encounter in just a few moments.

Trail Regions

- Mammoth Hot Springs and North Entrance Area
- Tower-Roosevelt, Lamar Valley, and Northeast Entrance Area
- Norris Area
- Madison and West Entrance Area
- Canyon Village and Grand Canyon of the Yellowstone River Area
- Old Faithful Area
- Fishing Bridge, Bridge Bay, Lake Village, Yellowstone Lake, and East Entrance Area
- West Thumb, Grant Village, Shoshone Lake, and South Entrance Area

Trail Ratings

Factors such as a trail's elevation profile, length, and obstacles determine its rating. The rating order used in this Fat Ass Guide is:

FAT ASS FRIENDLY Trails

Very Easy - trails under 1 mile (1.6 km) long with minimal elevation changes and minimal trail obstacles

Easy - trails between 1 mile (1.6 km) and 2.9 miles (4.7 km) long with minimal elevation changes and minimal trail obstacles

Moderately Easy - trails between 3 miles (4.8 km) and 5.9 miles (9.5 km) long with minimal elevation changes and minimal trail obstacles

Other Trails

Moderate - trails that either have prominent elevation changes between 100 feet (31 m) and 199 feet (61 m); are between 6 miles (9.7 km) and 8.9 miles (14.3 km) long; have some trail obstacles; or have a combination of these elements

Moderately Difficult - trails that either have prominent elevation changes between 200 feet (61 m) and 299 feet (91

m); are between 9 miles (14.5 km) and 11.9 miles (19.2 km) long; have some trail obstacles; or have a combination of these elements

Difficult - trails that either have prominent elevation changes between 300 feet (91 m) and 399 feet (122 m); are between 9 miles (14.5 km) and 11.9 miles (19.2 km) long; have some trail obstacles; or have a combination of these elements

Very Difficult - trails that either have prominent elevation changes between 400 feet (122 m) and 499 feet (152 m); are between 12 miles (19.3 km) and 14 miles (22.5 km) long; have some trail obstacles; or have a combination of these elements

FORGET IT, FAT ASS Trails

Strenuous - trails that either have prominent elevation changes over 499 feet (152 m); are over 14 miles (22.5 km) long; have many trail obstacles; or have a combination of these elements

It's no coincidence that many FORGET IT, FAT ASS trails include the words peak, mountain, ridge, and mount!

Coordinates

Coordinates listed at the end of each trail description may refer to that trail's trailhead, access point, a nearby parking lot, or a nearby pullout.

Mammoth Hot Springs and North Entrance Area

ROAD NOTE: Highway 89 between Yellowstone's North Entrance and Mammoth Hot Springs Village is open year-round. The road between Gardiner, MT and Cooke City, MT is open year-round.

Mammoth Area Highlights:

- Mammoth Hot Springs Terraces
- Fort Yellowstone Historic Buildings
- Boiling River Hot Water Swimming
- 45th Parallel

FAT ASS FRIENDLY Hikes In This Area:
(trail number and name)

1. Boiling River
2. Fort Yellowstone +
5. Lower Terraces ++
7. Wraith Falls

+ wheelchair and stroller accessible
++ wheelchair and stroller accessible - in parts

NOTE: Wheelchair rental is available at Mammoth Hot Springs Medical Clinic.

Information:

Park Information - 307-344-7381

- Albright Visitor Center & Museum

Located in Mammoth Hot Springs Village, Albright Visitor Center & Museum is open seven days a week, year-round. In the summer, a backcountry office in the visitor center issues camping, fishing, and boating permits. The museum hosts many history-related exhibits and famous works by artist-explorer Thomas Moran.

Medical Services:

Medcor operates a year-round clinic offering urgent care services in Mammoth Hot Springs. Hours of operation may vary.

Clinic information - 307-344-7965

Eats:

SUMMER OPTIONS

- Mammoth Hot Springs Hotel Dining Room
- Mammoth Hot Springs General Store (groceries)
- Mammoth Hot Springs Terrace Grill

WINTER OPTIONS

- Mammoth Hotel Dining Room
- Mammoth General Store (lunch on weekdays)

The Hikes:

1. Boiling River

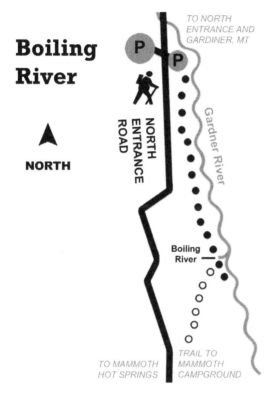

- Fat Ass Friendly
- Activity - Swimming

Take a dip in nature's original Jacuzzi on this easy half-mile (.8 km) out-and-back skip to a sweet spot where the sizzling runoff from nearby Mammoth Hot Springs mixes with the cool Gardner River to create a unique swimming hole. This is one of the few places in Yellowstone where you are allowed to hop in and enjoy the park's naturally heated water, so bring a swimsuit and towel, and thoroughly indulge in this extraordinary spa!

TRAIL NOTE: **BATHING SUIT, NOT BIRTHDAY SUIT!** This off-map trail is no secret, and the Boiling River sees hundreds of visitors per day during the summer. To protect this fragile area, the trail is only accessible during daylight hours. Pets, bikes, camping, food, beverages, soap, nudity, and off-trail hiking are prohibited. Double-check usability during late spring and early summer when snowmelt turns the Gardner River into a raging, quick-moving beast.

TRAIL NOTE: **LETHAL WATERS!** Many hydrothermal waters in Yellowstone contain organisms that can cause skin rashes, infections, meningitis, and Legionnaire's Disease. These organisms can be fatal. Don't dunk your head underwater, and don't inhale hydrothermal steam. Seek immediate medical help if you suspect you've been infected with a creepy-crawly.

Find the trailhead about 2.5 miles (4 km) south of Yellowstone's North Entrance, on North Entrance Road, at the pullout on the east side of the highway, south of the 45th Parallel sign noting the latitudinal halfway point between the Equator and the North Pole. Follow the level trail alongside the banks of the Gardner River through Gardner Canyon. Keep an eye out for bison and elk.

FIELD NOTE: **TRAPPER-KNOWN RIVER.** The Gardner River and nearby "misspelled" Gardiner, Montana take their names from Johnson Gardner, a notable Yellowstone trapper from the 1830s.

Just .8 miles (1.3 km) from the trailhead, arrive at the meeting of massive geothermal discharge from Mammoth Hot Springs with the Gardner River. Here, the Boiling River emerges from an underground channel and creates a six-foot-wide 140°F (60°C) thermal runoff stream. This stream flows over delicate travertine ledges into the much cooler Gardner River. (Immersion and wading in the stream is strictly forbidden.)

Prospective dippers will find a nice swimming area in the Gardner River, in an alcove cordoned by a rock wall. Watch your footing on the slippery rocks and slide into the warm waters. As you find the perfect soaking spot, take care to stay within the swimming area. The Gardner River beyond the rocky ledge is swift-moving.

Benches around the pool accommodate those wishing to watch rather than dip. In the water or out, notice how the hydrothermal spillovers have created a unique tropical microclimate of year-round insects, waterfowl, fish, and greenery thriving in the river's never-ending summer.

After you've gotten your fill of warm water luxury, return to the trailhead by the same route.

Length: 1 mile (1.6 km) - roundtrip
Estimated time: 20 minutes
Elevation change: minimal
Rating: easy
Challenges: strong currents, unstable rock ledges, slippery rocks, lethal organisms in thermal waters
Attractions: Boiling River, hot springs, swimming, Gardner River, bison, elk
Trailhead: On North Entrance Road, about 2.5 miles (4 km) south of the park's North Entrance, find parking areas on both sides of the highway, very close to the Montana and Wyoming border. The trailhead is just south of the 45th Parallel on the east side of the highway.
* In 2008 the Park Service moved the 45th Parallel sign one mile (1.6 km) north of the parking area, about 1,200 feet (366 m) from the actual parallel, to ease congestion near the Boiling River from visitors seeking photo ops.
Coordinates: 44.992465, -110.691354

2. Fort Yellowstone Historic Trail

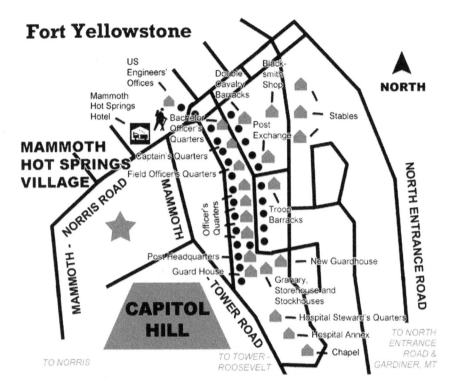

- Fat Ass Friendly
- Wheelchair and Stroller Accessible
- Self-Guided Trail

Explore Yellowstone's fascinating park beginnings on a very easy quarter-mile (.4 km) stroll among the historical buildings of Fort Yellowstone, right in Mammoth Hot Springs. A National Historic Landmark District, Fort Yellowstone Historic Trail guides visitors through the US Army's role in preserving Yellowstone National Park as a national treasure. Interpretive signs along the trail highlight the years between 1886 and 1913 when most of buildings were constructed to accommodate US Army troops stationed in the park.

FIELD NOTE: **SEND IN THE ARMY!** Before the creation of the National Park Service, the US Army managed Yellowstone's livelihood. The Army came to the park in 1886 to restore order to a land overrun with lawless poachers, timber cutters, prospectors, squatters, and vandals. In 1918 administration and control of Yellowstone finally fell into the hands of the newly formed Park Service, which was better equipped to deal with visitors' needs.

Find Fort Yellowstone Historical Trail in Mammoth Hot Springs Village, across from Mammoth Hot Springs Hotel and near the Albright Visitor Center. The buildings are grouped together and are noticeable by their stone structures and red roofs.

The trail includes views of Officer Row, the Guardhouse, the Chapel, the Troop Barracks, the Post Exchange, and many other buildings. In modern times, Fort Yellowstone remains integral to the park's infrastructure and is home to park headquarters.

Length: .25 miles (.4 km) - roundtrip
Estimated time: 30 minutes to 1 hour
Elevation change: minimal
Rating: very easy
Attractions: Fort Yellowstone, historical buildings, self-guided trail
Trailhead: in Mammoth Hot Springs Village, across from Mammoth Hot Springs Hotel and near Albright Visitor Center; look for the group of buildings with red roofs
Coordinates: 44.976897, -110.700426

3. Beaver Ponds

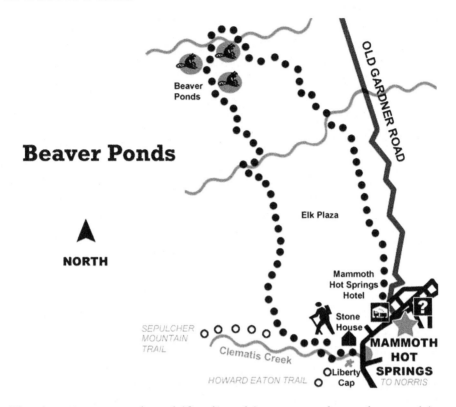

The beavers may be shifty but big game abounds on this difficult but very scenic 5-mile (8.1 km) loop trail through beautiful meadows and forests to a group of beaver-dammed ponds. Beaver Ponds makes a great spring hike as it is passable earlier than other areas of Yellowstone.

TRAIL NOTE: **PREPARE FOR BEARS!** This trail may be periodically closed due to bear activity. Check current trail availability at any visitor center. Use prudence, practice bear safety, and carry bear pepper spray when hiking this trail!

Find the trailhead just north of Mammoth Hot Springs Terraces (see **5. Lower Terraces**), on the west side of Mammoth - Norris Road, between Liberty Cap hot spring cone and the Stone House. Head west on Beaver Ponds - Sepulcher Mountain Trail, following Clematis Creek up the gulch. The creek was named for area clematis, a flowering plant of the buttercup family.

In .2 miles (.3 km) bear right at Howard Eaton Trail junction to stay on Beaver Ponds Trail. Cross a footbridge over the creek, enjoy the shade of fir trees, and hoof it up a strenuous 350-foot (107 m) climb with the help of some switchbacks.

At the Sepulcher Mountain Trail split, less than a mile (1.6 km) from the trailhead, follow the trail to the right (north) to stay on Beaver Ponds Trail. Continue through lovely meadows, watching for black bears, mule deer, elk, moose, and early summer wildflowers. Hike through conifer stands and sagebrush fields, and take in nice views of Mammoth Hot Springs and Fort Yellowstone.

Cross a footbridge over a small stream, and about midway along the loop, see ponds, lodges, and dams created by enterprising beavers. Notice trees chewed by the animal's massive incisors. As the trail descends to the rush-lined ponds, watch for waterfowl paddling about the tranquil waters.

FIELD NOTE: **ROBUST RODENT.** Beavers are part of the rodent family, the largest order of mammals. Rodents, characteristically known for their gnawing talents, have perpetually growing incisors but no canine teeth.

Continue traversing footbridges over streams along the loop, and head south through fir and poplar stands. Follow the trail along Elk Plaza, an open sagebrush plateau popular with elk, pronghorn, and other quick-hoofed creatures. Catch stunning views of the Absaroka Mountain Range, Sepulcher Mountain, Mount Everts, Bunsen Peak, and Mammoth Hot Springs Village.

Close to Mammoth, the trail follows alongside Old Gardiner Road, an old stagecoach route. Continue on the path to the end of the trail behind Mammoth Hotel. Bear right (southwest) for a short stroll back to the trailhead near Liberty Cap.

Length: 5 miles (8.1 km) - roundtrip
Estimated time: 2 to 3 hours
Elevation change: 450 feet (137 m)
Rating: difficult
Challenges: 350-foot (107 m) ascent, bears

Attractions: beavers, beaver ponds, dams, lodges, elk, mule deer, moose, pronghorn, black bears, wildflowers, creeks, Mount Everts, Sepulcher Mountain, Bunsen Peak, Absaroka Mountain Range

Trailhead: Beaver Ponds - Sepulcher Mountain - Clematis Gulch Trail, between Liberty Cap hot spring cone and the Stone House, next to Mammoth Hot Springs Terraces

Coordinates: 44.97307, -110.704025

4. Narrow Gauge Terrace

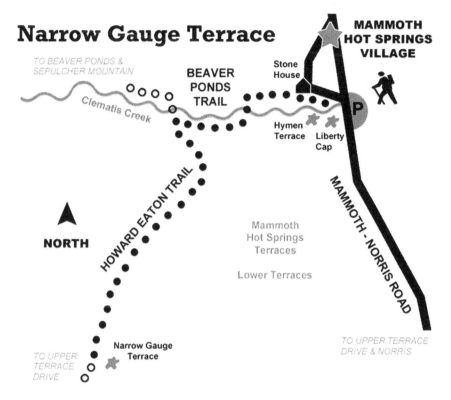

Move beyond Mammoth's massive crowds for an off-boardwalk tour of some of the world's rarest travertine terraces. This short, difficult one-mile (1.6 km) out-and-back hike is an adventurer's dream, crossing a creek, climbing through forests and sagebrush, and exploring a hidden treasure of ornate rock ledges blooming from misty hot pools.

TRAIL NOTE: **TOO HOT TO TROT!** Stay on trails in hydrothermal areas to prevent injury to yourself and avoid damage to the environment! Solid-looking ground may really be thin crusts hiding very hot water capable of causing third-degree burns and even death! Constantly changing landscapes make off-trail travel extremely dangerous!

Find the trailhead just north of Lower Terraces (see **5. Lower Terraces**), on the west side of Mammoth - Norris Road, between Liberty Cap hot spring cone and the Stone House. Head west on Beaver Ponds - Sepulcher Mountain Trail.

Immediately look to the left of the trail to see Hymen Terrace, this walk's first travertine feature.

FIELD NOTE: **BATH TENT!** Yellowstone's first bathhouse was built in a tent pitched over a hole fed by thermal waters near Hymen Terrace. Natural hot spring baths were very popular in the late 1800s for their touted healing properties. Unfortunately, human manipulation of Yellowstone's hydrothermal features often led to irrevocable environmental damage and was ultimately discontinued to protect and preserve the park's unique resources.

Past the steam-shrouded terrace, catch a glimpse of Historic Fort Yellowstone and the sedimentary walls of 7,841-foot (2,390 m) Mount Everts.

FIELD NOTE: **MELTED MOUNTAIN OF FOSSILS!** Mount Everts, named for 1870's explorer Truman Everts, was once buried under glacial ice. Hydrothermal activity melted the ice, leaving behind mounds of glacial debris (kames). The mountain's sandstone and shale layers are a result of an inland sea that washed over the area about 70 to 140 million years ago. The sea deposited fossils in the mountain's steep slopes. The mountainside is also packed with cultural artifacts left by The Sheep Eaters, an ancient people who followed bighorn sheep migrations through Yellowstone.

Follow Clematis Creek as it winds along the northern edge of Lower Terraces and through a forest of mixed pine and aspen. Keep an eye out for elk and bears nosing about these cool stands. Cross Clematis Creek via a small footbridge. In .2 miles (.3 km) arrive at Howard Eaton Trail junction. Bear left towards Narrow Gauge. (The trail to the right leads to **3. Beaver Ponds**.)

Climb through coniferous forests and open sagebrush flats as the trail ascends 240 feet (73 m) over .3 miles (.5 km). Periodic trail users will note hot features frequently appear, disappear, and move locations altogether in this highly active hydrothermal area. Most interestingly, water quantities remain relatively constant here as energy transfers to activate one feature while simultaneously deactivating another.

Arrive at Narrow Gauge Terrace, a raised travertine bed on the left side of the trail. Continue down the trail for a closer look at the terraces, a fantastical creation steaming hot pool waters and framed by dead, leached trees. Note the colorful streaks decora travertine. This indicates the presence of thermophiles water-loving bacteria).

FIELD NOTE: **RARE TERRACES.** Active travertine terraces are very rare. Hundreds of millions of years ago, a sea covered the Mammoth Hot Springs area and the shells from marine organisms formed a layer of limestone (calcium carbonate). Present-day subterranean waters carry dissolved calcium carbonate to the spring's surface where it releases carbon dioxide to create white, calcareous travertine rock.

Narrow Gauge hike ends here. Retrace your steps back to the trailhead.

Length: 1 mile (1.6 km) - roundtrip
Estimated time: 2 hours
Elevation change: 360 feet (110 m)
Rating: difficult
Challenges: 360-foot (110 m) ascent over a half mile (.8 km), hydrothermal area
Attraction: Narrow Gauge Terrace
Trailhead: Beaver Ponds - Sepulcher Mountain - Clematis Gulch Trail, between Liberty Cap hot spring cone and the Stone House next to Mammoth Hot Springs Terraces
Coordinates: 44.97307, -110.704025

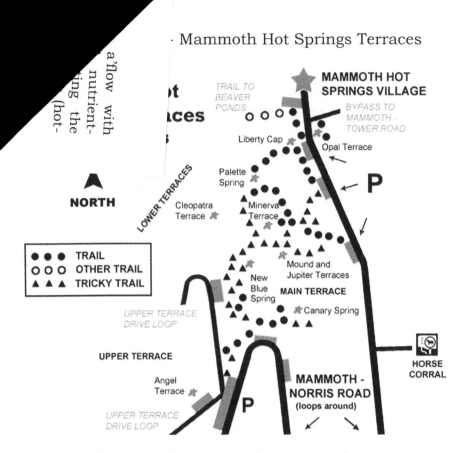

- Fat Ass Friendly - to Opal Terrace, Liberty Cap, and Palette Spring; to Minerva Terrace; and to Canary Spring
- Wheelchair and Stroller Accessible - in parts
- Attractions - Opal Terrace, Liberty Cap, Minerva Terrace, Cleopatra Terrace, Mound Terrace, Jupiter Terrace, New Blue Spring, and Canary Spring
- Self-Guided Trail

Walk a wonderland of strangely beautiful, alien-like landscapes on an easy-to-difficult boardwalk stroll around some of the most unique hydrothermal features in the world. Interpretive signs along the trail illuminate the inner-workings of this extremely rare place of active travertine terraces. Because the terraces of Mammoth Hot Springs are continually evolving systems, pick up a trail guide at the trailhead for the most up-to-date routes.

TRAIL NOTE: **TOO HOT TO TROT!** Stay on boardwalks in hydrothermal areas to prevent injury to yourself and avoid damage to the environment! Solid-looking ground may really be thin crusts hiding very hot water capable of causing third-degree burns and even death! Constantly changing landscapes make off-trail travel extremely dangerous!

Find the Lower Terraces boardwalk entrances at the parking areas at the south end of Mammoth Hot Springs Village.

FIELD NOTE: **HOT SPRINGS BRIMSTONE.** While the Lewis and Clark Expedition never passed through Yellowstone, their maps show the route that trapper John Colter took through the area in 1807. Colter called the area "Hot Springs Brimstone."

Begin the hike at the northern-most parking area by Liberty Cap hot spring cone and Opal Terrace for the most comprehensive tour of Lower Terraces. The trails to Opal Terrace, Liberty Cap, and Palette Spring are wheelchair and stroller accessible.

FIELD NOTE: **THERMAL TERRACES.** Mammoth's thermal waters are believed to travel north from Norris by way of a fault line. In Mammoth these hot waters stream through limestone (calcium carbonate) deposits. Water carries dissolved calcium carbonate to the spring's surface and releases carbon dioxide to form Mammoth's famous white travertine terraces. In most other areas in Yellowstone, hot spots pass through smooth, bulging rhyolitic lava flows, which are almost the antithesis of the intricately sculpted travertine ledges of the Mammoth Hot Springs area.

On the east side of the road, across from Liberty Cap and the Stone House, is Opal Terrace. Opal Terrace is an interesting example of a prioritizing push and pull faced by the National Park Service in protecting both natural resources and historic institutions. Once a dormant pool, Opal Spring bubbled to life in 1926; as a result, travertine began to build up and dramatically alter the now-developed area. In the late 1940s, in order to accommodate the evolving terrain, a nearby tennis court was dismantled. Today, Opal Terrace is encroaching on a historic home designed by famed architect Robert Reamer. Sandbags and a wall protect this early 1900's treasure but one has to wonder whether Opal Terrace will eventually reclaim that lot as well.

From Opal Terrace, cross over to the west side of the street to see Liberty Cap. (The unpaved trail to the north of Liberty Cap leads to **3. Beaver Ponds**.) Liberty Cap is a dormant, 37-foot (11 m) cone formed from deposits carried up from a hot spring over hundreds of years. It is named for the pointed hats symbolizing liberty worn during the French Revolution. From Liberty Cap, continue west on the trail to chromatic Palette Spring. Many colored heat-loving bacteria (thermophiles) cling to the tiered limestone hillside here, bathing in the hot thermal waters that trickle down the slope.

For the fattest-ass friendly tour of Lower Terraces, backtrack to the parking lot and move your vehicle two parking lots south, to the area just north of the horse corral. Note that Lower Terraces is a very popular trek and parking may often be limited. If you decide to walk the rest of Lower Terraces, understand that the trail has a 300-foot (91 m) elevation gain over the chalky white terraces to its southern end on Upper Terrace Drive.

From the south parking lot, follow the stroller-and-wheelchair-accessible boardwalk northwest to Minerva Terrace. Bear right at the first junction. (The trail to the left leads up to Mound and Jupiter Terraces.) Bear left at the next junction. (The trail to the right leads down to the middle parking area.) Cross over a steep boardwalk that heads north-south and continue west to Minerva Terrace.

FIELD NOTE: **SKELETON TREES.** Keep your eye out for odd white-banded bobbysoxed trees dotting the travertine flows of Lower Terrace. Calcium carbonate deposits from thermal waters overtook the tree stands, ringing their trunks in white shackles and effectively smothering the life out of them.

On the east side of the trail, see the elaborate 30-foot (9 m) ledges of Minerva Terrace, named for the Roman goddess of artists and handicrafts. The vivid sculpture-like travertine steps of this Yellowstone favorite are a wonderful illustration of the changing nature of thermal areas. Minerva has undergone periods of activity and inactivity, transforming parched platforms to slick steps and vice versa; in fact,

Minerva changes so rapidly that it may be virtually unrecognizable from one generation to the next. The elevated boardwalk here accommodates the massive quantity of minerals deposited by the hundreds of gallons of water that flow over Minerva's intricate ledges each minute.

To continue the fattest-ass tour of Lower Terraces, backtrack from Minerva Terrace to the parking lot and drive south on Mammoth - Norris Road to Upper Terrace Drive. Bear right on Upper Terrace Drive and follow the one-way loop to the first pullout on the left side of the road. Take the stroller-and-wheelchair-accessible boardwalk on the right side of the road to bright yellow Canary Spring. Note that this route will bypass the more challenging, but beautiful, features of Cleopatra Terrace, Mound Terrace, Jupiter Terrace, and New Blue Spring.

For the hard-ass tour of Lower Terraces, from Minerva Terrace continue on the boardwalk as it bends northwest and loops south. Here, the boardwalk parallels the forest and climbs to steamy Cleopatra Terrace on the west (right) side of the trail. Cleopatra's striking orange and white hues are due to colonies of bacteria that thrive in the warm water cascading over the rock ledges.

Next up, see Jupiter Terrace and Mound Terrace. Currently dormant, Mound Terrace was once known for its striking prism of colors, while Jupiter's heavy gushings swamped boardwalks in the 1980s. Backtrack up to the intersection and turn left (southwest) to view colorful, changing New Blue Spring. From New Blue Spring, hike south to the pullout on Upper Terrace Drive. (The one-way road at Upper Terrace Drive loops counterclockwise around other notable Mammoth terraces.) Catch your breath at the Overlook, and marvel at the magnificent pastel travertine staircases descending to Mammoth Village beneath glittering, snowy mountain peaks.

At the southeast end of the Upper Terrace Drive pullout, pick up the spur boardwalk and walk east along the southern edge of Main Terrace. Don't let the flat, table-like travertine structure of Main Terrace fool you. This rapidly changing feature may appear radically different with each visit. Continue east on the boardwalk to see Canary Spring, so named for the bright yellow sulfur-loving bacteria living in this hot pool's waters. Lower Terraces trail ends here. Retrace your steps back to your preferred trailhead.

Length: 1.5 miles (2.4 km) - roundtrip
Estimated time: 2 hours
Elevation change: 300 feet (91 m)
Rating: easy to difficult
Challenges: 300-foot (91 m) ascent from Lower Terraces' north end to its south end at Upper Terrace Drive; hydrothermal area
Attractions: Opal Terrace, Liberty Cap, Palette Spring, Minerva Terrace, Cleopatra Terrace, Jupiter Terrace, Mound Terrace, New Blue Spring, Main Terrace, Canary Spring, self-guided trail
Trailhead: at the south end of Mammoth Hot Springs Village, at the parking areas on the west side of Mammoth - Norris Road, before
the horse corral
Coordinates: 44.972829, -110.703995 or 44.971387, -110.703329 or 44.9695, -110.702256 (Lower Terraces parking areas)

Mammoth Hot Springs Terraces © Christina Myers

6. Hoodoos - of Terrace Mountain

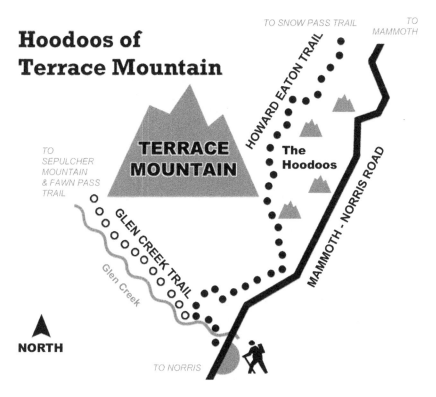

Journey through strange geology on a moderately difficult 3-mile (4.8 km) hike up Terrace Mountain to a ghostly land of ancient travertine blocks. Along the trail, enjoy excellent views of radiant Golden Gate Canyon.

Find the Glen Creek trailhead at the pullout on the west side of Mammoth - Norris Road, 5 miles (8.1 km) south of Mammoth Hot Springs Village. Follow Fawn Pass - Glen Greek Trail west across Glen Creek to Howard Eaton Trail junction. Bear right on Howard Eaton Trail. (To the left, Fawn Pass - Glen Creek Trail leads to Sepulcher Mountain and Snow Pass Trail.) Like a primordial guard, Terrace Mountain rises 8,006 feet (2,440 m) to overlook the intersecting trails.

FIELD NOTE: **ANCIENT HOTSPOT.** Terrace Mountain is the oldest thermal area in the park. It is an enormous travertine terrace, just like Mammoth Hot Springs Terraces (see **5.**

Lower Terraces), though Terrace Mountain is now dormant. This incredible mountain is at least 406,000 years old!

Follow Howard Eaton Trail northeast as it plows through burned forests up the side of Terrace Mountain. This marks the beginning of a one-mile (1.6 km) climb, 250 feet (76 m) up and over the hillside, to the hoodoos. Take frequent breaks and enjoy the view. Look to the right (east) to see the shimmering sides of Golden Gate Canyon. Its orange lichen walls appear to crack the earth wide open as Glen Creek tumbles over Rustic Falls.

Continue on the trail as it descends to the hoodoos. 1.5 miles (2.4 km) from the trailhead, enter an other-word of eerie white boulders strewn about the mountainside. These blocks are known as hoodoos.

FIELD NOTE: **HOODOO VOODOO**. Hoodoos are columns or pinnacles of weathered rock. In this case, the odd rock formations of Terrace Mountain are not technically hoodoos but rather travertine stacks that just plain look hoodoo-y strange. Travertine is formed when hydrothermal water brings dissolved calcium carbonate to the earth's surface, where it releases carbon dioxide and creates the white rock.

Meander about the odd rocks, and return to the trailhead by same the route. (The trail beyond the hoodoos leads north to Mammoth Hot Springs and west to Snow Pass Trail.)

Length: 3 miles (4.8 km) - roundtrip
Estimated time: 1 to 2 hours
Elevation change: 250 feet (76 m)
Rating: moderately difficult
Challenges: 250-foot (76 m) ascent over 1 mile (1.6 km) and returning descent
Attractions: hoodoos, Terrace Mountain
Trailhead: Glen Creek - Fawn Pass Trail, at the pullout on the west side of Mammoth - Norris Road, 5 miles (8.1 km) south of Mammoth Hot Springs Village
Coordinates: 44.931285, -110.729479

Wraith Falls

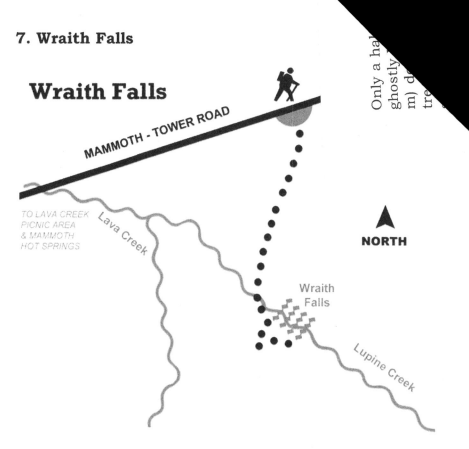

- Fat Ass Friendly

Get out of the car and stretch your legs on this short-and-easy one-mile (1.6 m) roundtrip stroll to Wraith Falls, a pretty cascade just off the main drag, on Lupine Creek.

Find the trailhead on Mammoth - Tower Road, about 5 miles (8.1 km) east of Mammoth Hot Springs and a quarter mile (.4 km) west of Lava Creek Picnic Area, at the pullout on the south side of the highway.

From the trailhead, follow the recently restored trail down a boardwalk and over a dirt path through wetlands, wildflower fields, sagebrush meadows, and pine forests. Watch for birds, elk, bison, and bears while enjoying wonderful views of Mount Sepulcher and Electric Peak. Cross a rambling stream by way of a footbridge, and walk up a short set of stairs to a viewing platform at the foot of Wraith Falls.

mile (.8 km) from the trailhead, snowmelt creates Wraith Falls cascade. The waterfall flows 100 feet (31 own Blacktail Deer Plateau and jettisons around fallen s on Lupine Creek. The falls are most dramatic in the snowmelts of early summer. After frolicking about the falls, return to the trailhead by the same route.

Length: 1 mile (1.6 km) - roundtrip
Estimated time: 30 minutes
Elevation change: minimal
Rating: easy
Attraction: Wraith Falls
Trailhead: on Mammoth - Tower Road, about 5 miles (8.1 km) east of Mammoth and .25 miles (.4 km) east of Lava Creek Picnic Area, at the pullout on the south side of the road
Coordinates: 44.942305, -110.623465

FORGET IT, FAT ASS Hikes In This Area:

- ## Lava Creek

Tumble almost 800 feet (244 m) down Lava Creek Canyon to the base of Mount Everts, dodging bighorn sheep and waterfalls along the way, on this strenuous 3.5-mile (5.6 km) one-way shuttle hike across the Gardner River to Mammoth Campground.

- ## Sepulcher Mountain

This scarily grueling, often-snowy 11-mile (17.7 km) trek features a 3,400-foot (1,036 m) scramble up Sepulcher's summit. Like a herald, Sepulcher Mountain is named for the hoodoos (columns or pinnacles of weathered rock) on its peak. The hoodoos resemble sepulchers, or monuments cut in rock in which a dead person is laid or buried.

- ## Bunsen Peak

This 4.2-mile (6.8 km) wallop up to the top of an old volcano shoots hikers 1,300 feet (396 m) over summer snowfields to the 8,564-foot (2,610 m) apex of Bunsen Peak. Pay homage to pioneering Icelandic geyser researcher Robert Wilhelm Bunsen at the peak, among park telecommunications equipment and spellbinding mountain views.

- ## Osprey Falls

Navigate narrow, dangerous switchbacks as this 8-mile (12.9 km) heart-pumper descends 700 feet (213 m) into awesome Sheepeater Canyon to a powerful 150-foot (46 m) waterfall. Dodge falling rocks and slippery footing along the way.

- ## Rescue Creek

A steep 1,500-foot (457 m) descent marks this 8-mile (12.9 km) one-way popular spring wildlife safari through sagebrush, forests, and meadows; past kettle lakes, and across the Gardner River. Rescue Creek is mistakenly named for explorer Truman Everts of the Washburn Expedition. In

1870 Everts became separated from his party and gear and wandered in the wilds for 37 days, living off of roots before being rescued near Tower Creek.

• **Blacktail Deer Creek - Yellowstone River**

Blacktail Deer Creek leads hikers 1,100 feet (335 m) down Black Canyon to the mighty Yellowstone River and into Gardiner, Montana on a 12-mile (19.3 m) one-way trek over sometimes slippery terrain.

Tower-Roosevelt, Lamar Valley, and Northeast Entrance Area

ROAD NOTE: The road between Gardiner, MT and Cooke City, MT, including Tower-Roosevelt, is open year-round.

Tower Area Highlights:

- Wolves
- Large Wild Bison Herd
- Large Elk Herd
- Lamar Valley and the Northern Range
- Basalt Columns from Lava Flows
- Waterfalls, Tower Fall

FAT ASS FRIENDLY Hikes In This Area:
(trail number and name)

8. Forces of the Northern Range +
14. Tower Fall ++

+ wheelchair and stroller accessible
++ wheelchair and stroller accessible - in parts, with assistance

Information:

Park Information - 307-344-7381

- Tower Ranger Station

Located in Tower Junction, Tower Ranger Station issues backcountry and fishing permits.

- Lamar Buffalo Ranch Ranger Station

Located in the Lamar Valley, Lamar Buffalo Ranch Ranger Station provides emergency services only.

- Northeast Entrance Ranger Station

Located at Yellowstone's Northeast Entrance, Northeast Entrance Ranger Station distributes important visitor information.

Eats:

SUMMER ONLY

- Roosevelt Lodge Dining Room
- Tower Fall General Store (groceries, restaurant)

THE HIKES:

8. Forces of the Northern Range

- Fat Ass Friendly
- Wheelchair and Stroller Accessible
- Self-Guided Trail

Families with kids will love this short, very easy .8-mile (1.3 km) roundtrip interpretive loop hike along the Forces of the Northern Range boardwalk. Exhibits illuminate the interplay between the powerful natural forces that shape the Yellowstone River and Lamar River landscapes. Benches along the loop provide convenient resting spots for leisurely travelers.

FIELD NOTE: **FORMERLY FIRE TRAIL.** After devastating wildfires tore through the park in 1988, children from around the world made donations to Yellowstone. Their generosity prompted the creation of this trail, which was initially called "The Children's Fire Trail." In 2003 the trail was renamed "Forces of the Northern Range" to highlight a broader focus on the Northern Range's special ecosystem.

This trail provides excellent opportunities to learn about volcanoes, glaciers, and wildfire while ambling among scorched pines and new growth forests. Signposts along the trail explain the relationships between animals of this region and their open range environment as low elevation and reduced snowpack provide excellent winter grazing habitats for large game and ample hunting opportunities for their predators.

FIELD NOTE: **BIG GAME.** Some of the world's largest free-roaming bison and elk herds are found in the sprawling grasslands of Yellowstone's Northern Range.

Length: .8 miles (1.3 km) - roundtrip
Estimated time: 30 minutes
Elevation change: minimal
Rating: very easy
Attractions: self-guided trail, the Northern Range
Trailhead: 8 miles (12.9 km) east of Mammoth Hot Springs on Mammoth - Tower Road, on the north side of the highway
Coordinates: 44.959423, -110.566605

9. Garnet Hill

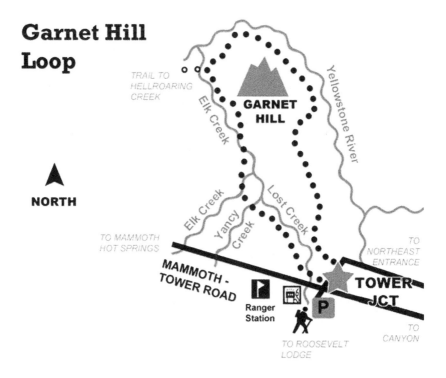

Garnet Hill Loop

Discover the jewel of Yellowstone's Northern Range on a very difficult 7.5-mile (12.1 km) loop hike around rocky Garnet Hill. Ramble along a stagecoach road, through bison territory, and into the wild habitats of the mighty Yellowstone River. Lower elevation and early snowmelt make Garnet Hill an excellent choice to both kick off and conclude the hiking season.

TRAIL NOTE: **WHOA HORSES!** The southern part of this trail is a major thoroughfare for Roosevelt Lodge horse happenings. If you encounter horseback riders, horse-drawn coaches, or any type of horse activity, calmly move off the trail so that the parties may pass.

Find the Garnet Hill Loop trailhead on the west side of Northeast Entrance Road, about 50 yards (46 m) north of Tower-Roosevelt Junction. Follow the flat dirt trail along a stagecoach route. Pass Lost Creek, and watch for herds of bison and elk afoot in the open sagebrush-speckled meadows of Pleasant Valley.

Follow the southern banks of Lost Creek as it winds through the valley, along the western edge of Garnet Hill. 1.5 miles (2.4 km) from the trailhead, reach an old cookout spot. Cross Yancy Creek once and Elk Creek twice, heading north alongside Elk Creek's eastern banks. Look for evidence of beaver activity, including creek-side beaver ponds.

Amble through shady wooded glens to a meadow, keeping a keen watch for bears in these idyllic wilds. About 4 miles (6.4 km) from the trailhead, just before the trail meets the mighty Yellowstone River, arrive at a trail junction. Bear right (east) to stay on Garnet Hill loop. (The path to the left leads west to scary Hellroaring Trail.)

Bend northeast on a picturesque tract between the Yellowstone River and the north face of Garnet Hill. Fishermen's trails lead down to the river but just keep right to follow Garnet Hill loop as it bends south through a valley on the mount's eastern edge. Press on through pine forests, and hike switchbacks partially up and around Garnet Hill, climbing 450 feet (137 m) over one mile (1.6 km). Keep an eye out for marmots at play on the mount's rocky slopes.

FIELD NOTE: **GEM MOUNTAIN.** Garnet Hill is named for rough garnets found in the mineral assemblages of its rocks.

The trail does not summit Garnet Hill. It eventually descends back through wildflowers and sagebrush rippling towards the southeastern Lamar River - Yellowstone River confluence and its Specimen Ridge backdrop. At the next trail junction, bear left to join a well-trod horse trail back to Northeast Entrance Road. Bear right (southwest) on Northeast Entrance Road, and walk a quarter mile (.4 km) to the Tower Junction service station parking area.

Length: 7.5 miles (12.1 km) - roundtrip
Estimated time: at least 4 hours
Elevation change: 450 feet (137 m)
Rating: very difficult
Challenges: 450-foot (137 m) ascent over 1 mile (1.6 km), horse activity

Attractions: Garnet Hill, Elk Creek, Yellowstone River, grazing bison, bears, marmots

Trailhead: Find Garnet Hill Loop Trail on the west side of Northeast Entrance Road, about 50 yards (46 m) north of Tower Junction. Parking is available in the large parking area east of the Tower Junction service station.

Coordinates: 44.915852, -110.416387

10. Lost Lake

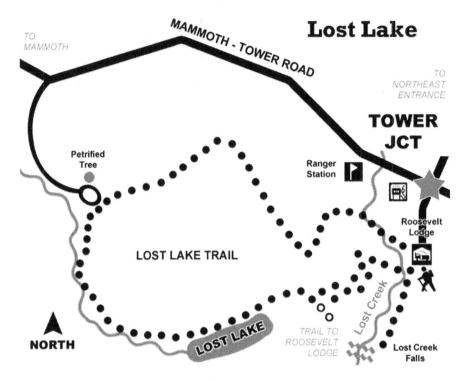

* Attraction - Petrified Tree

Discover the charm of a hidden lake on a difficult 4-mile (6.4 km) roundtrip loop hike past a waterfall, through a forest, and over a hillside to lily-padded Lost Lake. Continue the adventure with a visit to fascinating fossilized Petrified Tree on this tour of the mysteries of Tower Junction.

TRAIL NOTE: **WHOA HORSES!** Horse activity is common in this area. If you encounter horses, horseback riders, or any type of horse activity, calmly move off the trail so that the parties may pass.

Find the trailhead in Tower-Roosevelt Junction, on the south side of the highway, behind Roosevelt Lodge. Choose the southernmost trailhead for a clockwise loop around Lost Lake. (The northern trailhead leads directly to Petrified Tree.)

Follow the trail west to Lost Creek Falls Trail. To the left, a short .2-mile (.3 km) one-way spur trail leads south to Lost Creek Falls, a 40-foot (12 m) waterfall nestled in a dark, narrow canyon. Bear right (west) at the junction to stay on Lost Lake Trail. Follow Lost Lake Trail as it crosses a footbridge over Lost Creek. For the next .6 miles (1 km) hike through a thick, rocky forest, climbing 350 feet (107 m) up steep switchbacks. On a ledge above the hillside, bear right (west) at the next trail junction to stay on Lost Lake Trail.

Continue on Lost Lake Trail for .2 miles (.3 km). Traverse wetlands, and arrive at the northern banks of lily pad-speckled Lost Lake. Amble along its peaceful shores, watching for black bears, moose, beavers, and waterfowl. Follow the trail as it bends north along a creek and passes through stands of aspens and firs. As the creek skirts west away from the trail, reach Petrified Tree.

FIELD NOTE: **PETRIFIED!** Petrified Tree is a fossil of an old redwood. 45 - 50 million years ago, the tree was buried by fast-moving silica-rich volcanic deposits and mudflows. These mineral-rich deposits helped preserve and petrify the tree. The protective iron fence around the tree helps deter illegal vandalism and sneaky fossil hunting.

At the northeast end of the parking lot, pick up the trail and climb 200 feet (61 m) up a hill. Watch for birds of prey on the grassy, sagebrush-dotted plateau. Delight in fantastic views of the Absaroka Range and the Beartooth Mountains as the path descends back to Tower Junction. Sneak behind Tower Ranger Station and the Tower maintenance area, and cross Lost Creek once again. Watch for orange markers signaling the trail's exit by the cabins at Roosevelt Lodge.

Length: 4 miles (6.4 km) - roundtrip
Estimated time: 2 to 3 hours
Elevation change: 600 feet (183 m)
Rating: difficult
Challenges: 350-foot (107 m) ascent, 200-foot (61 m) ascent, bears, horse activity, trail finding
Attractions: beavers, black bears, Lost Lake, Petrified Tree,
Trailhead: in Tower Junction, behind Roosevelt Lodge
Coordinates: 44.912715, -110.416707

11. Yellowstone River Picnic Area

Climb where the bighorn sheep be on a very difficult 3.7-mile (6 km) roundtrip loop hike along a canyon rim above the Yellowstone River. Along the way, enjoy excellent views of the canyon's Narrows, Overhanging Cliff, and landmark Bannock Ford.

TRAIL NOTE: **WATCH YOUR STEP!** Loose rocks, steep drop-offs, and vertigo views require extra care when hiking this trail!

Find the trailhead at Yellowstone River Picnic Area, 1.25 miles (2 km) east of Tower Junction, on the east side of the parking lot. Follow the trail as it rolls 200 feet (61 m) over a hill and through pines along the eastern rim of the Grand Canyon of the Yellowstone River. The canyon in this area is only 400 feet (122 m) deep and is known as The Narrows. The views here are wonderful with the Absaroka Mountain range chiseling the sky to the east and Mount Washburn rising to -

the south. Notice evidence of glaciation. Massive boulders (erratics) tossed this way and that across the land are due to an old retreating glacier.

At a top of the craggy shelf, continue southeast along the trail, watching for resplendent bighorn sheep climbing steep bluffs. Keep an eye out for eagles, osprey, and falcons soaring in the canyon. At the far side of the plateau, take a peek at the mighty Yellowstone River carving the canyon walls. Across the river, wonder at the towering basalt columns of Overhanging Cliff. These columns were formed by cooling lava.

Look south to spot the convergences of Tower Creek and Antelope Creek with the Yellowstone River. Beyond the creeks as the river bends southeast, note a small island. This is the famed Bannock Ford, where the Bannock Indians would cross the river during buffalo hunts.

Follow the trail as it descends to Specimen Ridge Trail, and bear left (north) on Specimen Ridge Trail. Hike a mile (1.6 km) through forests and meadows lush with spring wildflowers. When the trail meets Northeast Entrance Road, bear left (west) and hike .7 miles (1.1 km) back to Yellowstone River Picnic Area.

Length: 3.7 miles (6 km) - roundtrip
Estimated time: 2 to 3 hours
Elevation change: 580 feet (177 m)
Rating: very difficult
Challenges: 400-foot (122 m) ascent, vertigo views
Attractions: bighorn sheep, birds of prey, Yellowstone River, Overhanging Cliff, Bannock Ford
Trailhead: at Yellowstone River Picnic Area on Northeast Entrance Road, 1.25 miles (2 km) east of Tower Junction, on the south side of the road.
Coordinates: 44.916867, -110.40055

12. Slough Creek

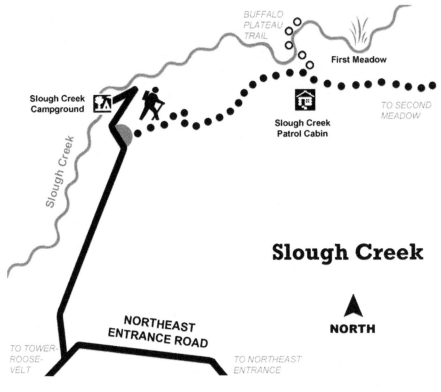

Slough Creek

NORTH

- Activity - Fishing

Unleash your inner cowboy and unreel your slick fisherman on this very difficult 4-mile (6.4 km) to 7-mile (11.3 km) out-and-back hike along an old wagon trail to the paradise-like meadows of trout-laden Slough Creek.

BEFORE YOU GO: **FISHING PERMITS.** All anglers must have Yellowstone Fishing Permits. All Yellowstone visitor centers, ranger stations, and general stores issue fishing permits. Tower Ranger Station is the closest permitting office to Slough Creek trailhead.

TRAIL NOTE: **WHOA HORSES!** Horses and horse-drawn wagons use these trails as a primary supply route to historic Silver Tip Ranch. If you encounter horses, horseback riders, or any type of horse activity, calmly move off the trail so that the parties may pass.

TRAIL NOTE: **PREPARE FOR BEARS!** This trail enters a key bear habitat. Use prudence, practice bear safety, and carry bear pepper spray when hiking this trail!

TRAIL NOTE: **BITING INSECTS!** Swarms of bloodthirsty mosquitoes invade wet river meadows in summer. Arm yourself with insect repellant!

Find Slough Creek trailhead on the gravel access road to Slough Creek Campground, off of Northeast Entrance Road, about 6 miles (9.7 km) east of Tower Junction. From the trailhead, follow the rutted wagon trail as it bumps 400 feet (122 m) over a mile (1.6 km) through mixed forests. Pass summer wildflowers and big boulders courtesy of the last Ice Age. Continue on the trail as it winds through wetlands often filled with moose.

Slough Creek Trail eases up, descending into idyllic Slough Creek valley along a bend in Slough Creek. Slough Creek is a world-class cutthroat trout stream, drawing fly fishermen by the flock to angle for the elusive fish. Continue along Slough Creek Trail to the sweeping First Meadow. The First Meadow is a great place to relax and have a snack among the lovely scenery. Don't get too comfortable! Elk and grizzlies are known to also enjoy this grassy slice of Eden.

About 2 miles (3.2 km) from the trailhead, Slough Creek intersects with Buffalo Plateau Trail. Buffalo Plateau Trail bows left (north) and crosses Slough Creek, which can be dangerous with snowmelt in spring and early summer. To the right of Slough Creek Trail is a backcountry patrol cabin.

If you'd like to hike to the Second Meadow, continue east on Slough Creek Trail. Climb 200 feet (61 m) up a hill, and in 1.5 miles (2.4 km) reach the Second Meadow. Whether your destination is the First Meadow or the Second Meadow, return to the trailhead by the same route.

Length: 2 miles (3.2 km) to the First Meadow; 3.5 miles (5.6 km) to the Second Meadow - one-way
Estimated time: 1 to 3 hours - one-way
Elevation change: 400 feet (122 m)
Rating: very difficult

Challenges: 400-foot (122 m) ascent over 1 mile (1.6 km), bears, bugs, horse activity
Attractions: grizzly bears, moose, wagon trail, Slough Creek, fishing
Trailhead: 6 miles (9.7 km) east of Tower Junction, on Northeast Entrance Road, head north on the gravel road to Slough Creek Campground. The trailhead is located where the road bears left (northwest) by the campground entrance.
Coordinates: 44.943567, -110.308134

Slough Creek © Taseret - Dreamstime.com

13. Trout Lake

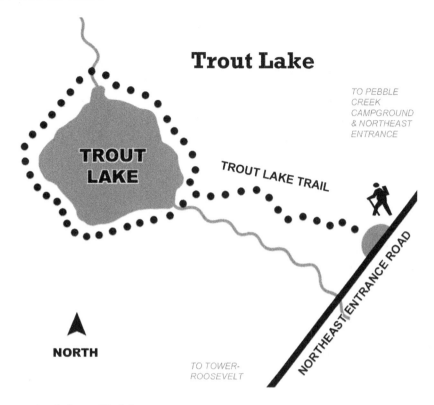

Trout Lake

TROUT LAKE

TROUT LAKE TRAIL

TO PEBBLE CREEK CAMPGROUND & NORTHEAST ENTRANCE

NORTHEAST ENTRANCE ROAD

NORTH

TO TOWER-ROOSEVELT

- Activity - Fishing

Visit a beautiful mountain lake filled to the gills with succulent trout on a moderately difficult 1.5-mile (2.4 km) walk to... Trout Lake, of course. This short hike provides wonderful opportunities to see a myriad of wildlife in a gorgeous mountain setting. Plenty of resting places along the lake trail make it a great picnic destination.

BEFORE YOU GO: **FISHING PERMITS.** Trout Lake, a former fish hatchery, is a very popular fishing hole full of cutthroat trout and rainbow trout. All anglers must have Yellowstone Fishing Permits. All Yellowstone visitor centers, ranger stations, and general stores issue fishing permits. Tower Ranger Station is the closest permitting office to Trout Lake.

TRAIL NOTE: **PREPARE FOR BEARS!** This trail enters a key bear habitat. Use prudence, practice bear safety, and carry bear pepper spray when hiking this trail!

Find the trailhead at the turnout just south of Pebble Creek Campground, on the north side of Northeast Entrance Road, about 17 miles (27.4 km) east of Tower Junction. Follow the nicely maintained foot trail though a forest of mixed conifers, and climb about 200 feet (61 m) up switchbacks to the top of a small ridge. Gaze down on shallow 12-acre (5 hectare) Trout Lake, which is settled between 9,583-foot (2,921 m) behemoth Druid Peak to the northwest and striking 10,404-foot (3,171 m) Barronette Peak to the northeast.

Follow the trail to the southern shores of the Trout Lake, about .3 miles (.5 km) from the trailhead. At the junction bear either right or left as the path continues in a short, mostly level loop around the lake. Look for otters, beavers, ducks, and trout-loving bears in the jungle-y vegetation along the shoreline. Return to the trailhead by the same route.

Length: 1.5 miles (2.4 km) - roundtrip
Estimated time: 1 hour
Elevation change: 200 feet (61 m)
Rating: moderately difficult
Challenges: 200-foot (61 m) ascent and descent, bears
Attractions: Trout Lake, trout, fishing, bears, otters, beavers, waterfowl
Trailhead: 17 miles (27.4 km) east of Tower Junction, on Northeast Entrance Road, at the turnout just south of Pebble Creek Campground
Coordinates: 44.899149, -110.123139

14. Tower Fall

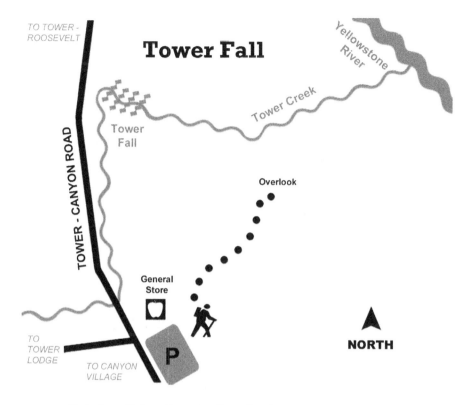

- Fat Ass Friendly - to Overlook
- Wheelchair and Stroller Accessible - with assistance, to Overlook
- Attraction - Tower Fall

Catch a glimpse of historic Tower Fall, the elegant waterfall that enchanted early park explorers and named the region, from a convenient viewing platform 100 very easy yards (91 m) from Tower Fall General Store. More adventuresome hikers can venture further on a short, steep trek to where Tower Creek tumbles into the Yellowstone River, on a difficult one-mile (1.6 km) roundtrip hike.

TRAIL NOTE: **PARTIAL CLOSURE.** Due to dangerous rockslides and mudslides that damaged portions of the trail and the lower viewing platform, the final third of the half-mile (.8 km) trail down to the base of Tower Fall is closed until further notice. Regardless of the length of your hike, watch your step as the trail may be slippery.

Find Tower Fall trailhead 2.5 (4 km) miles south of Tower-Roosevelt Junction, on the east side of the road at the Tower Fall General Store parking area. Follow the paved incline 100 yards (91 m) up to Tower Fall Overlook for a view of the top of the waterfall.

FIELD NOTE: **LAVA FLOW FALLS.** The Tower-Roosevelt area is the site of an old lava flow, evident in the columns of slowly cooled lava rock stacking about the region. Named for the basalt pinnacles decorating its crest, Tower Fall tumbles 132 feet (40 m) in a graceful column of water as Tower Creek flows over worn-away bedrock. An enormous boulder perched at the brink of the falls until June of 1986, when it finally toppled into the canyon.

The trail past the overlook winds down an ethereal landscape of delicate-yet-rocky forests to the picturesque confluence of Tower Creek and the Yellowstone River. The original trail descended 300 feet (91 m) over a half mile (.8 km) by way of switchbacks to the base of the falls. Today, the final third of the trail is closed due to dangerous rock-and-mudslide damage. On the accessible parts of the trail, watch for bighorn sheep, black bears, and large birds of prey that inhabit the Tower region. After exploring Tower Fall, return to the trailhead by the same route.

Length: 200 yards (183 m) to 1 mile (1.6 km) - roundtrip
Estimated time: up to 45 minutes
Elevation change: minimal to overlook; 300 feet (91 m) to creek
Rating: very easy to difficult
Challenges: 300-foot (91 m) descent and returning ascent to creek
Attraction: Tower Fall
Trailhead: 2.5 miles (4 km) south of Tower-Roosevelt Junction, on the east side of the road, at the Tower Fall General Store parking area
Coordinates: 44.891925, -110.386771

Tower Fall © Svetlana Foote - Dreamstime.com

FORGET IT, FAT ASS Hikes In This Area:

- ### Pebble Creek

Warm Creek. Pebble Creek. Upper Meadows. Beware of the deceptively charming names and seemingly convenient campground conclusion of this arching 12-mile (19.3 km) shuttle trek. Hikers hurtle 1,000 feet (305 m) over 1.5 miles (2.4 km) past alluring mountain peaks to a wildflower-filled glaciated valley and across an oft-dangerous creek with fast-moving water to Pebble Creek Campground.

- ### Petrified Trees

The stuff of nightmares, 1.5-mile (2.4 km) Petrified Trees Trail and its severe 1,200-foot (366 m) ascent rife with loose rocks leads hikers to stone-entombed trees fossilized by ancient lava flows. Those who dare to take the challenge will be accompanied by stunning views of the Lamar Valley.

- ### Specimen Ridge

Everything an exhausting hike should be, this difficult all-day 17.7-mile (28.5 km) shuttle hike along Specimen Ridge includes a 3,364-foot (1,025 m) ascent up 9,614-foot (2,930 m) Amethyst Mountain. Challenging terrain, a 2,854-foot (870 m) descent to a unique view of the Lamar Valley, and a roaring river crossing complete this hike.

- ### Hellroaring

Hell isn't sparked on this hike without reason - this extremely punishing 4-mile (6.4 km) roundtrip character builder includes disorienting trail junctions, a wickedly steep descent to Hellroaring Creek, infernal summer weather, and hard-to-come-by drinking water. Hear that? It's hell roaring because this hike's so damnably hard!

• Mount Washburn

Don't let the popularity of this postcard-perfect hike fool you! This 3.1-mile (5 km) (via Dunraven Pass) or 2.5-mile (4 km) (via Chittenden Road) leg burner delivers a strenuous 1,400-foot (427 m) ascent up an old rickety road to the summit of Mount Washburn, Yellowstone's primary fire lookout. Tempestuous weather and high altitudes add extra excitement for hike darers.

Norris Area

ROAD NOTE: Highway 89 between Mammoth Hot Springs and Norris is closed from early November until mid-April.

Norris Area Highlights:

- Steamboat Geyser
- Artists Paintpots
- Geothermal Features

FAT ASS FRIENDLY Hikes In This Area:
(trail number and name)

17. Norris Geyser Basin
18. Artists Paintpots ++

++ wheelchair and stroller accessible - in parts

Information:

Park Information - 307-344-7381

- Norris Geyser Basin Museum and Information Station

Located .25 miles (.4 km) east of Norris Junction, at the spur road to Norris Geyser Basin and Steamboat Geyser, Norris Geyser Basin Museum houses exhibits on geothermal activity, while the Information Station distributes important visitor information.

T#E #IKES:

15. Grizzly Lake

- Activity - Fishing

Venture where the brook trout bite on this moderately difficult 4-mile (6.4 km) out-and-back hike to Grizzly Lake, a 148-acre (60 hectare) lake nestled in a narrow valley in the shadow of Mount Holmes. Nearby creeks provide excellent spawning environments for trout, which take advantage of favorable inlets and outlets to bountifully populate Grizzly Lake's shimmering waters. Indeed, at Grizzly Lake, you're much more likely to encounter fish than bears.

BEFORE YOU GO: **FISHING PERMITS.** All anglers must have Yellowstone Fishing Permits. All Yellowstone visitor centers, ranger stations, and general stores issue fishing permits.

Find the trailhead on the west side of Mammoth - Norris Road, about 6 miles (9.7 km) north of Norris, and a mile (1.6 km) south of Beaver Lake Picnic Area. Follow Grizzly Lake Trail northwest across Obsidian Creek, through a lush meadow bursting with summer wildflowers. Climb switchbacks 250 feet (76 m) up to the top of a ridge. Notice many downed trees and twice-burnt conifers along the way. These trees are victims of both the 1976 and 1988 Yellowstone wildfires.

Atop the rolling ridge enjoy views of 10,336-foot (3,150 m) Mount Holmes and the Gallatin Mountain Range. In the valley below, long Grizzly Lake stretches between two slopes, pooling amid Straight Creek's channel. Follow switchbacks down the trail to the northern shores of Grizzly Lake. Explore the woodsy shoreline or try your luck with the trout. The hike ends here. Return to the trailhead by the same route.

(The trail beyond Grizzly Lake eventually intersects with Mount Holmes Trail. This difficult route requires a logjam crossing, presses through soggy marshes, and is often swarming with bloodthirsty mosquitoes.)

Length: 4 miles (6.4 km) - roundtrip
Estimated time: 2 to 3 hours
Elevation change: 250 feet (76 m)
Rating: moderately difficult
Challenges: marshy areas, steep climbs
Attractions: Grizzly Lake, brook trout, fishing, moose, elk, mountain views
Trailhead: on the west side of Mammoth - Norris Road, about 6 miles (9.7 km) north of Norris, and 1 mile (1.6 km) south of Beaver Lake Picnic Area
Coordinates: 44.800337, -110.74569

16. Solfatara Creek

Solfatara
Creek

NORTH

- Shuttle Hike

Appreciate the trail less trekked on this very difficult 6.5-mile (10.5 km) one-way shuttle hike along Solfatara Creek through obsidian-strewn land to a series of vibrant geothermal springs. Park a car at the ending trailhead to create a shuttle, or hike back on the same route to the trailhead.

TRAIL NOTE: **PREPARE FOR BEARS!** This trail enters a key bear habitat and may be periodically closed due to bear activity. Check current trail availability at any visitor center. Use prudence, practice bear safety, and carry bear pepper spray when hiking this trail!

TRAIL NOTE: **TOO HOT TO TROT!** Stay on trails in hydrothermal areas to prevent injury to yourself and avoid damage to the environment! Solid-looking ground may really be thin crusts hiding very hot water capable of causing third-degree burns and even death. Constantly changing landscapes make off-trail travel extremely dangerous!

Find the trailhead at the C loop of Norris Campground. Follow the trail north along bubbly Solfatara Creek, through a pine forest. At the Howard Eaton - Ice Lake Trail junction, keep left (northwest) to continue on Solfatara Creek Trail. (The trail to the right leads to Ice Lake.)

FIELD NOTE: **VILE VENTS!** A solfatara is a large volcanic area venting sulfurous gasses.

Trek over hills and through meadows for about 3 miles (4.8 km) to foul-smelling, brimstone-y Whiterock Springs. Continue northwest along the trail, and climb up to Lake of the Woods, a small lake tucked beyond the trail to the north. Carefully follow the somewhat scruffy and remote path through pine forests. Pass beguiling Amphitheater Springs and Willy Wonka-ish Lemonade Creek. For anyone thinking of pulling an Augustus Gloop and sneaking a taste, understand that geothermal features are uber-dangerous! Hike just a little further to the trail's end on the east side of Mammoth - Norris Road, about .75 miles (1.2 km) south of Beaver Lake Picnic Area.

Length: 6.5 miles (10.5 km) - one-way
Estimated time: 3 to 4 hours
Elevation change: 400 feet (122 m)
Rating: very difficult
Challenges: 400-foot (122 m) ascent and descent, bears, trail finding, trail length
Attractions: Lake of the Woods, geothermal springs, grizzly bears, obsidian
Trailhead: Norris Campground at the C loop
Coordinates: 44.738425, -110.692216

17. Norris Geyser Basin - Porcelain Basin Loop and Back Basin Loop

- Fat Ass Friendly - to various features
- Attraction - Steamboat Geyser
- Self-Guided Trails

Don't sweat the hottest area in Yellowstone! Easy boardwalks and trails loop among the volatile thermal landscapes of popular Norris Geyser Basin. .75-mile (1.2 km) Porcelain Basin Loop explores the pulsing barren landscape around enigmatic Black Growler Steam Vent, while 1.5-mile (2.4 km) Back Basin Loop leads to spectacular Steamboat Geyser, the tallest active geyser in the world.

TRAIL NOTE: **TOO HOT TO TROT!** Stay on boardwalks and trails in hydrothermal areas to prevent injury to yourself and avoid damage to the environment! Solid-looking ground may really be thin crusts hiding very hot water capable of causing third-degree burns and even death. Constantly changing landscapes make off-trail travel extremely dangerous!

Find the trailheads on the west side of Norris Junction, at the northwest end of the parking area by the Bookstore and Museum.

FIELD NOTE: **MAJOR FAULT AND A GUY NAMED NORRIS.** Norris Geyser Basin is named for Yellowstone's second park superintendent, Philetus W. Norris. Major fault lines intersect in this geyser basin to meet caldera-impacted fractures in the earth's crust. Precipitation caught in these crevices heats up and forms a boggling array hydrothermal hot springs, fumaroles, mudpots, and geysers.

Norris Geyser Basin -
Porcelain Basin Loop

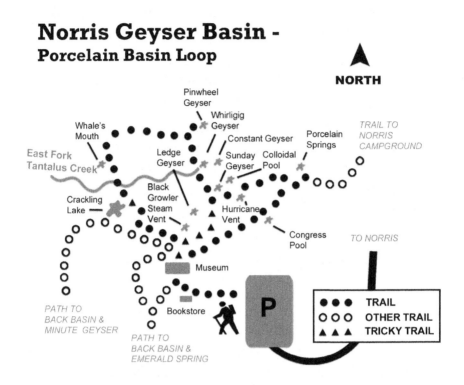

PORCELAIN BASIN LOOP: From the Museum, walk north on the trail past the three-way junction to Porcelain Basin Overlook. Notice the stark, acidic landscape buckling and bulging as hot pressurized water roils under white porcelain-like siliceous geyserite. Norris Geyser Basin is one of the most variable areas of Yellowstone with many features appearing from and disappearing into mysteriously changing chasms. The pungent smells in the basin are due to sulfurous gasses escaping from nearby geothermal vents.

FIELD NOTE: **YEARLY DISTURBANCES.** Every year around late summer and early fall, massive thermal upheavals rock Norris Geyser Basin for about a week. Calm pools may transform into erupting geysers and active geysers may fall all together silent. This odd annual phenomenon is unique to this geyser basin and its cause is unknown.

At the three-way junction, bear right (northeast) to steamy Congress Pool. (The trail to the left leads to Back Basin Loop. The trail straight ahead leads to Black Growler.) This calm turquoise pool occasionally transforms into a wildly boiling caldron when activated by area disturbances. Its name comes from the Fifth International Geological Congress, which met in Yellowstone in 1891.

Follow the trail northeast, and take the right spur to Porcelain Spring. The hard white mineral crusts here are siliceous sinter. Hot spring deposits may close up vents, causing pressurized water to erupt out of other fragile fissures.

FIELD NOTE: **SLOW BUILD.** Sinter builds up slowly over time, averaging less than an inch of accumulation per century. Imagine how long it must have taken to build the tall geyser cones seen throughout Yellowstone!

At Porcelain Spring, the trail to the right (east) leads to Norris Campground and the Museum of the National Park Ranger; instead, backtrack to the main trail and bear right to Hurricane Vent, a spitting fumarole. At the loop junction, bear right to Sunday Geyser and Colloidal Pool. (The trail to the left leads to Ledge Geyser and Black Growler Steam Vent.)

Continue north on the trail to Constant Geyser, which occasionally erupts in 30-foot (9 m) spurts, and Whirligig Geyser, a swirling splasher. Notice the ruddy color of Whirligig. This is caused by iron oxide deposits. Bear right on the short spur to Pinwheel Geyser overlook. Although Pinwheel is largely inactive, it sports a prismatic overflow channel alive with brightly colored thermophiles. These thermophiles thrive in hot, acidic water.

Return to the main loop. Bear right and head west. As the trail turns south, see Whale's Mouth, a cavity filled with hot water thought to resemble the mouth of a marine creature. Continue south on the boardwalk, and cross the East Fork of Tantalus Creek. Crackling Lake is up next on the right side of the trail. The lake takes it name from the sizzling sounds of nearby hot springs.

At the loop junction, bear left and climb down to vaporous Black Growler. (The trail to the right returns to the Museum.) Black Growler Steam Vent is a fumarole characteristically located on an incline above the area's water table. Fumaroles are the hottest of hydrothermal features, and Black Growler Steam Vent roasts between 199°F to 280°F (93°C to 138°C) hot. Most interestingly, Black Growler has a history of disappearing and reappearing in different places on the hill.

On the trail past Black Growler is Ledge Geyser, a large but irregular eruptor that projects water 125 feet (38 m) in the air. Turn around and climb back up the trail to the Museum to complete Porcelain Basin loop.

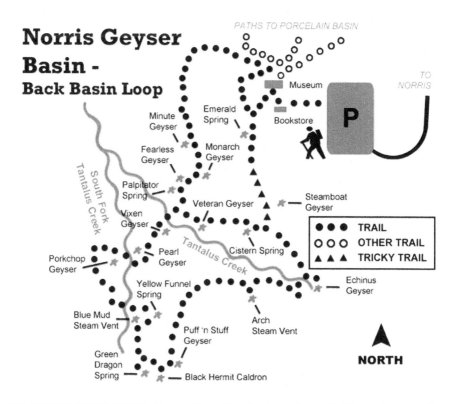

Norris Geyser Basin -
Back Basin Loop

PATHS TO PORCELAIN BASIN

Museum

Bookstore

P

TO NORRIS

Emerald Spring

Minute Geyser

Monarch Geyser

Fearless Geyser

Palpitator Spring

Steamboat Geyser

Veteran Geyser

Vixen Geyser

South Fork Tantalus Creek

Porkchop Geyser

Pearl Geyser

Cistern Spring

Tantalus Creek

Echinus Geyser

Yellow Funnel Spring

Blue Mud Steam Vent

Puff 'n Stuff Geyser

Arch Steam Vent

Green Dragon Spring

Black Hermit Caldron

● ● ●	TRAIL	
○ ○ ○	OTHER TRAIL	
▲ ▲ ▲	TRICKY TRAIL	

NORTH

BACK BASIN LOOP: From the Bookstore bear left on the trail, away from the Museum, to Emerald Spring. As the trail heads south and becomes a boardwalk, see the 27-foot (8 m) deep hot spring. Emerald Spring is coated with yellow sulfur deposits which blend with blue light reflected from the spring to create its rich emerald-green tones.

Negotiate stairs, climbing down uneven ground to Steamboat Geyser. Magnificent Steamboat Geyser is the tallest active geyser in the world. Rare 300-foot (91 m) eruptions rocket out of the geyser with deafening roars, showering the region with dazzling silica-rich water. In an hours-long encore, the geyser expels powerful blasts of steam high into the sky. Eruptions are highly unpredictable, with intervals ranging from 4 days to 50 years. Smaller bursts up to 40 feet (12 m) are more common.

Bear right at the loop junction for a look at deep blue Cistern Spring. (The trail to the left leads to Black Pit Spring.)

Thermal waters overflow from Cistern, quickly altering the landscape by flooding the forest with silica deposits. The white buildup around the trees' bases is known as a bobbysoxing. Cistern Spring is connected beneath the earth to Steamboat Geyser, and their behaviors operate in tandem. During or after major Steamboat eruptions, Cistern Spring completely drains.

Backtrack to the loop junction, and bear right to Black Pit Spring and Echinus Geyser. Crusty Echinus Geyser is the largest of the world's rare acid-water geysers. It has a pH of 3.3 to 3.6, about the same as vinegar. Echinus means sea urchin; indeed, the geyser's pinkish, spiny deposits do look rather urchin-y. Echinus Geyser is an irregular eruptor, with powerful 40- to 60-foot (12 to 18 m) explosion intervals ranging from hours to months.

Cross Tantalus Creek and follow the trail west, passing Arch Steam Vent and Mythic Spring. As the loop swings south, see Puff 'n' Stuff Geyser, a minor spitter, and Black Hermit Caldron. Follow the trail northwest to Green Dragon Spring, a hot spring sporting a mysterious steam-and-sulfur-filled cavern. The boardwalk levels out at murky Blue Mud Steam Vent and bubbling Yellow Funnel Spring. Follow the path north across the South Fork of Tantalus Creek.

Beyond the creek see Porkchop Geyser. Porkchop was once a small, noisy, occasionally erupting hot spring. On September 5, 1989, it violently exploded, hurling rocks more than 200 feet (61 m) into the air. Today, its waters gently simmer in its craggy pot.

Cross the creek fork again as the trail winds past colorful Pearl Geyser. See Vixen Geyser, a steaming, burbling chasm that occasionally spits out water. Past Vixen, cross Tantalus Creek, and bear right at the loop junction for a quick look at Corporal Geyser and Veteran Geyser. Backtrack to the loop junction, and bear right to Palpitator Spring. (The trail to the left returns to Vixen Geyser.) Gas bubbles rising from beneath the earth's surfaces make Palpitator beat like a heart. Follow the trail past Fearless Geyser to Monarch Geyser, a once violent geyser that is now an overflowing hot pool.

Continue to Minute Geyser and its foot-high roils, which are a sad testament to the effects of civilization on hydrothermal features. Yellowstone's main route once passed right by Minute Geyser and many past park visitors tossed objects into this lively feature. Minute's main vent became clogged, dampening regular 60-second 50-foot (15 m) high water blasts to small and irregular spurts. Follow the trail north and east to the Museum and Bookstore to complete Back Basin loop.

Length: .75 miles (1.2 km) (Porcelain Basin), 1.5 mile (2.4 km) (Back Basin) - roundtrip
Estimated time: 30 minutes (Porcelain Basin), 1 hour (Back Basin)
Elevation change: 100 feet (31 m), each loop
Rating: easy to moderate
Challenges: hydrothermal area, 100-foot (31 m) climbs
Attractions: Porcelain Basin, Back Basin, Black Growler Steam Vent, Steamboat Geyser, Echinus Geyser, hydrothermal features, self-guided trails
Trailhead: slightly west of Norris Junction
Coordinates: 44.725996, -110.701967

Norris Geyser Basin © Andrea Hornackova - Dreamstime.com

18. Artists Paintpots

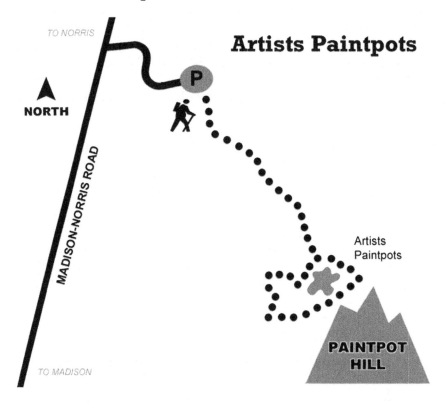

- Fat Ass Friendly
- Wheelchair and Stroller Accessible - to the base of Paintpot Hill

Fill the canvas of your imagination with delight in a fairytale of fantastical sputtering mudpots and other thermal oddities on this short one-mile (1.6 km) out-and-back loop hike around an oversized palette of striking pools in the lively Gibbon Geyser Basin.

TRAIL NOTE: **TOO HOT TO TROT!** Stay on boardwalks and trails in hydrothermal areas to prevent injury to yourself and avoid damage to the environment! Solid-looking ground may really be thin crusts hiding very hot water capable of causing third-degree burns and even death. Constantly changing landscapes make off-trail travel extremely dangerous!

Find the trailhead at the parking area on the east side of Norris - Madison Road, about 4.5 miles (7.2 km) south of Norris. Follow the boardwalk south through stands of lodgepole pines rejuvenating after the devastating 1988 wildfires, and pass by furtive volcanic vents. After a short walk about .3 miles (.5 km) from the trailhead, arrive at the base of Paintpot Hill, a lively mount bursting with thermal activity.

Bear left to begin the loop. Feast your eyes upon spectral pools soaking in rich reds to milky blues. Iron oxide, silica, and bacteria all contribute to the striking colors of these pools.

Continue on the trail, passing small geysers, and start a 60-foot (18 m) climb up the steamy slopes of Paintpot Hill. This part of the trail is short but steep, so you'll be huffing and puffing right along with the hill's fumaroles. Relax, take frequent breaks, and enjoy incredible views of the Gibbon Geyser Basin with its many wonders spread beneath the dominating crests of the Gallatin Mountain Range.

Keep on chugging to the masters of this domain, a pair of heaving mudpots. These aberrations right out of a storybook seem to almost enjoy belching odorous gas and chucking hot mud all over the place. Approach the mud-crusted platform nearest to the creature at your own risk.

FIELD NOTE: **MAKING MUDPOTS.** In mudpots, microorganisms convert thermal gas to sulfuric acid, which breaks down rhyolitic rock into clay. As gasses escape the mud, it bubbles and belches. The geothermal features of Artists Paintpots change seasonally. As precipitation falls and wanes, water seeps in and out of the ground, collecting and evaporating to create varying viscosities and behaviors. The mud may take the shape of soupy pots or solid cones.

Continue along the trail, descending past continually interesting spectral pools. The red pool on the eastern part of the trail is Blood Geyser, an occasionally erupting spring colored by bright iron oxide. Bear left at loop's close to return to the trailhead.

Length: 1 mile (1.6 km) - roundtrip
Estimated time: 30 - 45 minutes
Elevation change: 60 feet (18 m)
Rating: easy to moderate
Challenges: steep 60-foot (18 m) ascent, splattering mud, hydrothermal area
Attractions: mudpots, hot springs, small geysers, colorful pools, fumaroles
Trailhead: 4.5 miles (7.2 km) south of Norris on Norris - Madison Road, at the parking area on the east side of the highway
Coordinates: 44.696355, -110.741132

Artists Paintpots © Christina Myers

FORGET IT, FAT ASS Hikes In This Area:

• Monument Geyser Basin

This short 2-mile (3.2 km) colossus boasts a nearly 650-foot (198 km) clamber over a half mile (.8 km) through burned forests and over eroding volcanic rocks to secluded Monument Geyser Basin. The seldom-visited basin is home to beautiful mountain-and-river views and 10-foot (3 m) tall sputtering Monument Geyser cone.

• Mount Holmes

Don't do it, homes. This superhuman 3,000-foot (914 m) 19-mile (30.6 km) climb up to the gusty fire lookout summit of 10,336-foot (3,150 m) Mount Holmes requires barreling through expansive snow sweeps and either a night on the mountain or a return after dark. Yikes.

Madison and West Entrance Area

ROAD NOTE: Highway 20 from Madison to West Entrance (and onto West Yellowstone) is closed from early November until mid-April.

Madison Area Highlights:

- Madison River, Missouri River headwaters

FAT ASS FRIENDLY Hikes In This Area:
(trail number and name)

20. Two Ribbons +
21. Riverside

+ wheelchair and stroller accessible

Information:

Park Information - 307-344-7381

- Madison Information Station

Located in Madison Junction at Madison Picnic Area, the Madison Information Station distributes important information to park visitors.

- West Yellowstone Visitor Information Center

Located in the town of West Yellowstone, MT, the West Yellowstone Information Center distributes important information to park visitors.

THE HIKES:

19. Harlequin Lake

Escape the beaten path with a peaceful one-mile (1.6 km) out-and-back mosey to charming Harlequin Lake. With convenient highway access, this moderate hike is a wonderful diversion for wildlife watchers particularly interested in waterfowl.

TRAIL NOTE: **MARSH MADNESS!** Marshy lake areas attract biting mosquitoes. Arm yourself with insect repellant!

Find the trailhead and its register across the street from the secret Madison River turnout on West Entrance Road. Follow Harlequin Lake Trail north and west through badly burned forests and new small pine growths. Head west up a gentle 100-foot (31 m) ascent along the base of Purple Mountain, and descend through tranquil lake marshes. In a half mile (.8

km) find reeds and rushes swaying on the southern banks of secluded Harlequin Lake.

Lily pad-dotted Harlequin Lake is small, only 10 acres (4 hectares) in area, and rather shallow. Look for beavers, elk, an array of waterfowl, and the many bird species that call Harlequin Lake home. Oddly enough, Harlequin Lake does not host harlequin ducks. Enjoy this little slice of aquatic nirvana; then, return to the trailhead by the same route.

Length: 1 mile (1.6 km) - roundtrip
Estimated time: 30 minutes
Elevation change: 100 feet (31 m)
Rating: moderate
Challenges: bugs, 100-foot (31 m) ascent and returning descent
Attractions: beaver lodge, elk
Trailhead: 1.7 miles (2.7 km) west of Madison Junction, on the north side of West Entrance Road, across the street from the Madison River turnout
Coordinates: 44.640302, -110.887393

Two Ribbons

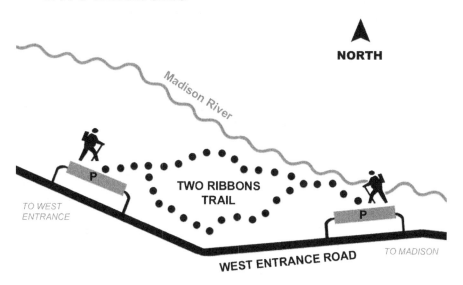

- Fat Ass Friendly
- Wheelchair and Stroller Accessible
- Self-Guided Trail

A wonderful introductory walk or wrap-up jaunt on your way through Yellowstone's West Entrance, very easy .75-mile (1.2 km) Two Ribbons Trail explores a forest thriving in the aftermath of an intense wildfire. This looping boardwalk ambles through regenerating woodlands and fields nestled between West Entrance Road and the Madison River.

Find the two parallel trailheads at the large pullouts on the north side of West Entrance Road, about 3 miles (4.8 km) east of West Entrance. The trail begins near the interpretive exhibits. From either trailhead, follow the boardwalk as it travels through a mosaic of burned, partially burned, and unburned forests. As wildfire swept through the area in

1988, changing winds and variable moisture content of the vegetation created a patchwork burn pattern. The result is a varied ecosystem capable of supporting a diverse mix of flora and fauna.

FIELD NOTE: **NEEDS HEAT!** Some lodgepole pinecones only open in intense heat. Wildfires open the cones and the seeds drop into the nutrient-packed, carbon-rich forest floor. On Two Ribbons Trail, young pines are regenerating under the open skies left behind by their fallen predecessors.

Take the return loop as it winds through flats of sagebrush and summer wildflowers along the sapphire-blue Madison River. Watch for bison, elk, coyotes, and owls.

FIELD NOTE: **BIG RIVER!** In Madison, the Gibbon River and the Firehole River meet to form the Madison River. The Madison River is one of three headwaters of the Missouri River. It joins the Gallatin River and the Jefferson River in Three Forks, Montana to form the Missouri River. In 1805 in Three Forks, Meriwether Lewis of the celebrated Lewis and Clark Expedition named the Madison River for then-Secretary of State James Madison. In 1809 James Madison became President of the United States.

Length: .75 miles (1.2 km) - roundtrip
Estimated time: 20 minutes
Elevation change: minimal
Rating: very easy
Attractions: Madison River, self-guided trail
Trailhead: 3 miles (4.8 km) east of West Entrance, at the two pullouts on the north side of the road
Coordinates: 44.652299, -111.03752 (west parking area); 44.651605, -111.030793 (east parking area)

Riverside

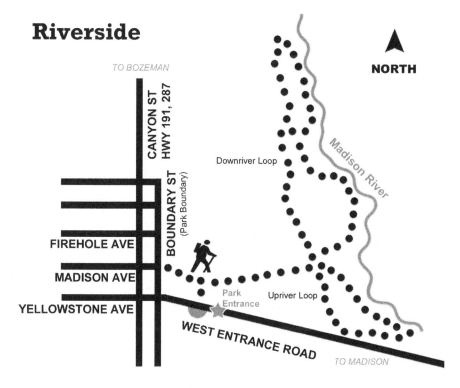

- Fat Ass Friendly - Multi-Mile Trail
- Activities - Fishing and Bicycling

A popular multi-use trail for all seasons, Riverside is a local favorite, leading hikers, bikers, skiers, and anglers along a relaxing path through the cool forests and beautiful meadows that flourish by the true-blue waters of the Madison River. With multiple trail lengths from 2.5 miles (4 km) to 4.5 miles (7.2 km) long, all flat and easy, Riverside is an excellent destination for both families with small children and laid-back adventurers.

Find the trailhead just west of Yellowstone's West Entrance, on the north side of the road across from the pullout. Follow the trail north for less than a quarter mile (.4 km), and bear right (east) at the junction. (The trail to the left leads to the West Yellowstone trailhead at Boundary Street and Madison

Avenue.) Continue on the trail as it meanders through lodgepole pine forests towards the Madison River. Keep an eye out for bison, deer, elk, moose, large birds of prey, and graceful water birds thriving in this excellent river habitat.

.75 miles (1.2 km) from the trailhead, arrive at the loops junction where the trail forms a figure eight of two loops - north and south - on a ledge above the Madison River. The loop to the left (north) is Downriver Loop, which is 2.3 miles (3.7 km) to 3.5 miles (5.6 km) long. The loop to the right (south) is Upriver Loop, which is 1.5 miles (2.4 km) long.

DOWNRIVER LOOP: Bear left (north) at the loop junction, and bear right again to follow the eastern-most loop along the Madison River as it winds through forests and open meadows bursting with spring wildflowers. Take in excellent Gallatin Mountain scenery and the soaring 10,336-foot (3,150 m) peak of Mount Holmes.

FIELD NOTE: **STAGECOACH STORAGE.** Note rugged Barns Hole Road, which runs from West Entrance Road to the gravel beds by the Madison River. Barns Hole, as the name suggests, was the site of many storage barns used by both park administrators and an old stagecoach depot.

Continue on Downriver Loop and arrive at a cutoff on the left side of the trail, which bends west and south for a shorter 2.3-mile (3.7 km) hike; otherwise, bear right at the cutoff for a full 3.5-mile (5.6 km) hike. Many trails along the Madison River follow old fish and game trails; likewise, Riverside provides excellent river access for fishermen angling for a catch.

Bear right again at the returning cutoff to stay on the main loop. Bear right at the loops junction to return to the trailhead or continue straight to explore Upriver Loop.

UPRIVER LOOP: At the loops junction, bear right (south) to Upriver Loop. Take the eastern-most trail for a counterclockwise loop that follows the Madison River to the southeast. Continue on the trail as it bends west and north to postcard views of the mighty mountain peaks of the Gallatin Range. Return to the loops junction. Bear left to return to the trailhead, or continue straight to explore Downriver Loop.

Length: 2.5 miles (4 km) to 4.5 miles (7.2 km) - roundtrip
Estimated time: 1 to 3 hours
Elevation change: minimal
Rating: easy
Attraction: Madison River, bicycling, fishing
Trailheads: Two trailheads lead to Riverside Trail. On West Entrance Road just west of the park entrance, find the trailhead on the north side of the road across the street from the turnout. In the nearby town of West Yellowstone, find the trailhead on the east side of Boundary Street at Madison Avenue.
Coordinates: 44.657069, -111.091468 (West Entrance Road) or 44.660311, -111.097216 (West Yellowstone, Boundary Avenue and Madison Avenue)

FORGET IT, FAT ASS Hikes In This Area:

- **Purple Mountain**

Take a good ol' fashioned 6-mile (9.7 km) roundtrip American challenge up a consistently steep, usually deserted trail to the top of 8,433-foot (2,570 m) Purple Mountain on an ambitious 1,600-foot (488 m) climb through thick lodgepole forests.

Canyon Village and Grand Canyon of the Yellowstone River Area

ROAD NOTE: The road between Tower Fall and Canyon Village, including the Grand Canyon of the Yellowstone River area, is closed from mid-October until late May.

Canyon Area Highlights:

- Grand Canyon of the Yellowstone River
- Scenic Rim Viewpoints
- Waterfalls
- Lakes

FAT ASS FRIENDLY Hikes In This Area:
(trail number and name)

22. Ice Lake - via Norris Road
27. Cascade Lake
28. North Rim of the Grand Canyon of the Yellowstone River - to Brink of the Upper Falls
29. South Rim of the Grand Canyon of the Yellowstone River - Artist Point to Sublime Point

Information:

Park Information - 307-344-7381

- Canyon Visitor Education Center

Canyon Visitor Education Center is located in Canyon Village. Exhibits explore volcanoes and geologic activity.

Eats:

SUMMER ONLY

- Canyon Lodge Cafeteria
- Canyon Lodge Dining Room
- Canyon Village General Store (groceries, restaurant)
- Canyon Village Outdoor Store (fast food, snacks)

THE HIKES:

22. Ice Lake - via Norris - Canyon Road

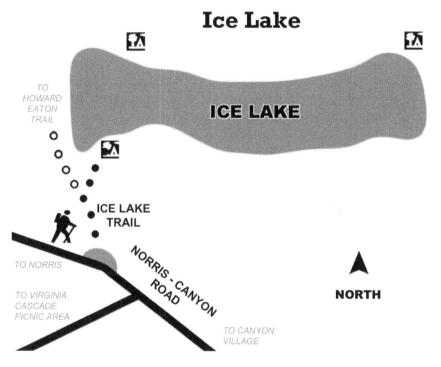

Ice Lake

ICE LAKE

TO
HOWARD
EATON
TRAIL

ICE LAKE
TRAIL

TO NORRIS

TO VIRGINIA
CASCADE
PICNIC AREA

NORRIS - CANYON
ROAD

TO CANYON
VILLAGE

NORTH

- Fat Ass Friendly
- Activity - Camping

Pack a picnic, bring the kids, and let grandma loose on this short, flat, very easy .3-mile (.5 km) one-way trek to small, peaceful Ice Lake. Beautiful backcountry scenery makes Ice Lake a wonderful introductory glimpse into Yellowstone's exciting outback.

BEFORE YOU GO: **CAMPING PERMITS.** Overnighters in Yellowstone's backcountry must have a Backcountry Use Permit. Campsite reservations may be made in advance. Canyon Visitor Education Center is the closest permitting office to Ice Lake's trailhead. Call 307-344-2160 or 307-344-7381 for more information. Prospective anglers should note that fish do not thrive in Ice Lake.

Find Ice Lake trailhead at the boardwalk by the turnout on the north side of Norris - Canyon Road, across the street from the end of the Virginia Cascade side road and picnic area. Follow the well-maintained, friendly-for-all trail for about .2 miles (.3 km) through a mixed conifer forest. Bear right at the spur, and arrive at the southern banks of Ice Lake.

Fallen lodgepole pines crisscross the terrain here in a noticeably lasting effect of the 1988 Yellowstone wildfires. This matrix of downed trees provides an important habitat for small animals, is a natural adventure spot for kids, and is a great place to enjoy a picnic. Relax on Ice Lake's tranquil shores, and watch for moose and elk hoofing around the area. Return to the trailhead by the same route.

CONTINUE THE ADVENTURE: From Ice Lake's trailhead, bear left at the spur junction to visit the lake's less-explored western banks. A half mile (.8 km) from the trailhead, meet Howard Eaton Trail, which leads left (west) to Norris Campground or right (east) to Wolf Lake, Grebe Lake, and Cascade Lake. (See **26. Howard Eaton Trail to... Norris Campground**.)

Length: .3 miles (.5 km) - one-way
Estimated time: 10 minutes
Elevation change: minimal
Rating: very easy
Challenge: fallen trees
Attractions: Ice Lake, camping, moose, elk, fallen logs, backcountry scenery
Trailhead: on Norris - Canyon Road, 3.5 miles (5.6 km) east of Norris, at the turnout on the north side of the highway, across the street from the end of the Virginia Cascade side road and picnic area
Coordinates: 44.716827, -110.633943

23. Little Gibbon Falls - via Wolf Lake - Ice Lake Trail Loop

- Activity - Camping

Romp about waterfall, river, and lake attractions on this moderate 3.9-mile (6.3 km) loop along the Gibbon River to Ice Lake. Convenient lakeside campsites transform this fun hike into a super-sweet overnight adventure.

BEFORE YOU GO: **CAMPING PERMITS.** Overnighters in Yellowstone's backcountry must have a Backcountry Use Permit. Campsite reservations may be made in advance. Canyon Visitor Education Center is the closest permitting office to Ice Lake's trailheads. Call 307-344-2160 or 307-344-7381 for more information. Prospective anglers should note that fish do not thrive in Ice Lake.

TRAIL NOTE: **BUGS 'N' MUD!** Wet river areas and lakeshores attract biting mosquitoes. Arm yourself with insect repellant, and use footwear capable of handling muddy conditions!

Find the trailhead on the north side of Norris - Canyon Road, at the orange markers across the highway from the end of the Virginia Cascade side road and picnic area. Follow oft-used, but poorly marked, Wolf Lake Cut-off Trail north along the Gibbon River.

FIELD NOTE: **EXPLORING THE GIBBON.** The Gibbon River was named for General John Gibbon, who explored this region in 1872. The Gibbon's headwaters include flows from nearby Grebe Lake, Wolf Lake, and Ice Lake.

Trek across the Solfatara Plateau, passing through meadows and lodgepole pine stands. Note the new growth landscape thriving in the wake of the fierce 1988 Yellowstone wildfires. See photo-ready Little Gibbon Falls, a 25-foot (8 m) cascade on the upper part of the Gibbon River. A few steps later, use a logjam to cross the Gibbon River. 1.3 miles (2.1 km) from the trailhead, arrive at Howard Eaton Trail junction. Bear left (west) towards Ice Lake. (The trail to the right heads northeast to Wolf Lake, Grebe Lake, and Cascade Lake.)

Negotiate another logjam and follow the western trail along the northern shores of pristine Ice Lake. In 1.5 miles (2.4 km) arrive at Ice Lake Trail junction. Bear right (south) towards Norris - Canyon Road. (The trail continuing east heads to Norris Campground.) Follow the developed path for a half mile (.8 km) along Ice Lake's western banks to Norris - Canyon Road. Walk left (east) along the road's wide shoulder for .6 miles (1 km). Arrive at Wolf Lake trailhead to complete the hike.

Length: 3.9 miles (6.3 km) - roundtrip
Estimated time: 2 to 3 hours
Elevation change: minimal
Rating: moderate
Challenges: bugs, mud, bad signage, trail finding, logjams, stream crossings
Attractions: Little Gibbon Falls, Gibbon River, Ice Lake, camping
Trailhead: on Norris - Canyon Road, about 4 miles (6.4 km) east of Norris, at the orange markers by the turnout on the north side of the highway, across the street from the end of the Virginia Cascade side road and picnic area
Coordinates: 44.71304, -110.628076

Cygnet Lakes

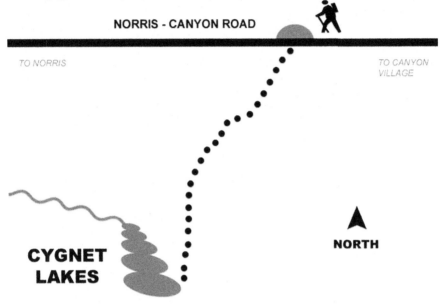

NORRIS - CANYON ROAD

TO NORRIS

TO CANYON VILLAGE

CYGNET LAKES

NORTH

- Bear Area

Visit a chain of five marshy lakes on a flat 8.2-mile (13.2 km) out-and-back stroll to Cygnet Lakes. This moderate trail is popular with wildlife watchers who tromp through this area of Yellowstone's Central Plateau to observe the park's most notorious creatures - bears.

TRAIL NOTE: **PREPARE FOR BEARS!** Cygnet Lakes Trail enters a key bear habitat and is a day-use-only area. Use prudence, practice bear safety, and carry bear pepper spray when hiking this trail!

* Cygnet Lakes Trail was conditionally closed in August, 2011 as officials investigated the death of a Michigan hiker who was fatally mauled by a bear. The bear was ultimately located, linked to another hiker's death, and killed. (See **DANGEROUSLY TRUE: MARY MOUNTAIN MAULING** and

DANGEROUSLY TRUE: TERROR ON WAPITI LAKE TRAIL.)

Find the Cygnet Lakes - Plateau trailhead on the south side of Norris - Canyon Road, at the pullout about 5.5 miles (8.9 km) west of Canyon Village. Follow the trail south through charred pine forests, casualties of the massive 1988 Yellowstone wildfires. Continue hiking through wetlands, past ponds, and along meadows overflowing with late spring wildflowers. 4.1 miles (6.6 km) from the trailhead, arrive at the southern portion of Cygnet Lakes.

FIELD NOTE: **CYGNET STATS.** Cygnet Lakes, a string of five lakes, takes its name from area swans and their young, called cygnets. The southernmost lake is the largest lake at 26 acres (11 hectares). The lakes are relatively shallow at less than 20 feet (6 m) deep.

Muck about the marshes, and return to the trailhead by the same route. (The trail beyond the southeastern section of Cygnet Lakes is not maintained.)

Length: 8.2 miles (13.2 km) - roundtrip
Estimated time: 3 to 4 hours
Elevation change: minimal
Rating: moderate
Challenges: bears, marshy areas, trail length
Attractions: Cygnet Lakes, bears, ponds
Trailhead: on Norris - Canyon Road, 5.5 miles (8.9 km) west of Canyon Village, at the pullout on the north side of the highway
Coordinates: 44.7036, -110.596343

Grebe Lake

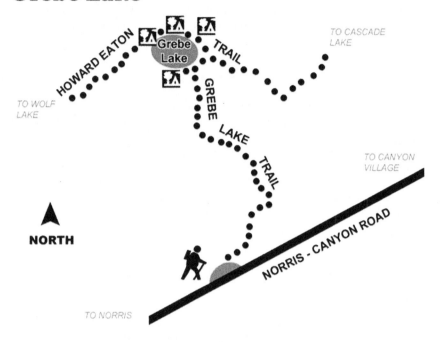

- Activities - Fishing and Camping

Strap your fishing pole to your pack for this moderate 6.6-mile (10.6 km) out-and-back jaunt to 156-acre (63 hectares) Grebe Lake, home to rare Arctic Grayling trout. Snow usually covers this trail until the end of June; otherwise, it's a very popular destination with anglers and backpackers.

BEFORE YOU GO: **CAMPING AND FISHING PERMITS.** Overnighters in Yellowstone's backcountry must have a Backcountry Use Permit. Campsite reservations may be made in advance. Canyon Visitor Education Center is the closest permitting office to Grebe Lake's trailhead. Call 307-344-2160 or 307-344-7381 for more information. All anglers must have Yellowstone Fishing Permits. All Yellowstone visitor centers, ranger stations, and general stores issue fishing permits.

TRAIL NOTE: **BITING INSECTS!** Wet lake areas attract bloodthirsty mosquitoes. Arm yourself with insect repellant!

Find Grebe Lake trailhead on Norris - Canyon Road, 3.5 miles (5.6 km) west of Canyon Village, at the pullout on the north side of the road.

FIELD NOTE: **WHAT'S A GREBE?** Grebe Lake was named by the United States Geological Survey of 1885 for the diving waterbird of the same name.

Follow Grebe Lake Trail north across the Solfatara Plateau, and head into Yellowstone's backcountry along an old road. A solfatara is an acidic volcanic crater emitting sulfurous gasses, so watch for gaseous volcanic openings in this area. Tromp through grassy meadows, past a pond, and into forests. Keep an eye out for elk, moose, and bears foraging in the new growth between wildfire-felled pines.

A little over 3 miles (4.8 km) from the trailhead, arrive at the southeastern shores of lily-pad-sprinkled Grebe Lake. Watch for osprey, pelicans, and ducks enjoying the lake's easy waters. Serious anglers will want to continue a bit farther north and west, bearing left at Howard Eaton Trail junction to the oxygenated waters of Grebe Lake's inlet and outlet. Here, Yellowstone-native Arctic Grayling, a strange fish with a dorsal fin, and rainbow trout wait for a bite. Return to the trailhead by the same route.

CONTINUE THE ADVENTURE: Howard Eaton Trail continues west (left) to Wolf Lake, Ice Lake, and Norris Campground; and east (right) to Cascade Lake and Observation Peak. (See **26. Howard Eaton to... Norris Campground**.)

Length: 6.6 miles (10.6 km) - roundtrip
Estimated time: 3 to 4 hours
Elevation change: minimal
Rating: moderate
Challenges: bears, bugs, early summer snowpack, trail length
Attractions: Grebe Lake, pond, bears, moose, elk, herons, fishing, rare Arctic Grayling, camping
Trailhead: on Norris - Canyon Road, 3.5 miles (5.6 km) west of Canyon Village, at the pullout on the north side of the road
Coordinates: 44.717237, -110.549592

26. Howard Eaton Trail - to Cascade Lake, Grebe Lake, Wolf Lake, Ice Lake, and Norris Campground

Howard Eaton Trail

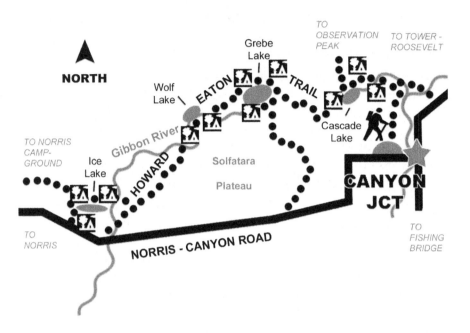

- Shuttle Hike
- Activities - Camping and Fishing

Take in Yellowstone's most tranquil backcountry lakes on this moderate-to-very-difficult 2.5-mile (4 km) to 12-mile (19.3 km) one-way shuttle hike down Howard Eaton Trail. Beautiful lakeside campsites along the trail and excellent fishing opportunities easily turn this walk into an irresistible backcountry adventure. Adventurers tackling all 12 miles (19.3 km) of the trail will need a shuttle (like a car) at the hike's end in Norris Campground.

BEFORE YOU GO: **CAMPING AND FISHING PERMITS.** Overnighters in Yellowstone's backcountry must have a Backcountry Use Permit. Campsite reservations may be made in advance. Canyon Visitor Education Center is the closest permitting office to this portion of Howard Eaton Trail. Call

307-344-2160 or 307-344-7381 for more information. All anglers must have Yellowstone Fishing Permits. All Yellowstone visitor centers, ranger stations, and general stores issue fishing permits.

TRAIL NOTE: **BUGS 'N' MUD!** Wet river areas and lakeshores attract biting mosquitoes. Arm yourself with insect repellant, and use footwear capable of handling muddy conditions on this river-crossing hike!

Find the trailhead a quarter mile (.4 km) west of Canyon Junction, on Norris - Canyon Road. Follow the trail north for 1.7 miles (2.7 km) along Cascade Creek, and bear left at the trail junction towards Cascade Lake. (The trail to the right heads to Cascade Lake Picnic Area.) Continue on the trail for .9 miles (1.5 km) and arrive at Cascade Lake's northern shores. (See **27. Cascade Lake**.) At the trail junction, keep left to stay on Howard Eaton Trail. (The trail to the right climbs steep switchbacks to Observation Peak.) Continue skirting the edge of the Solfatara Plateau to Grebe Lake.

FIELD NOTE: **MAKING A RIVER.** Grebe Lake, Wolf Lake, and Ice Lake are the headwaters of Yellowstone's mighty Gibbon River.

In 3.8 miles (6.1 km) reach Grebe Lake and Grebe Lake Trail junction. Bear right around Grebe Lake's northern shores. (See **25. Grebe Lake**.) (The trail to the left leads to Norris - Canyon Road.) Grebe Lake is an excellent place to angle for rare dorsal-finned Arctic Grayling and common rainbow trout.

Wade across the Gibbon River, and wind through marshes on the southern periphery of Wolf Lake. Watch for moose and sandhill cranes hiding in the rushes. Navigate occasionally unstable river logjams, and carefully follow a sometimes-faint trail to Ice Lake. Bear right at the trail junction to follow Howard Eaton around the northern shores of the lake. (The trail to the left leads to Little Gibbon Falls.) Bear right again at Ice Lake Trail junction. (The trail to the left leads to Norris - Canyon Road.) Hike through meadows and pine forests. Cross Solfatara Creek to arrive at the eastern edge of Norris Campground, the hike's conclusion.

Length: 2.5 miles (4 km) to Cascade Lake, 4.25 miles (6.8 km) to Grebe Lake, 6.25 miles (10.1 km) to Wolf Lake, 8.25 miles (13.3 km) to Ice Lake, 12 miles (19.3 km) to Norris Campground - one-way
Estimated time: 3 to 8 hours
Elevation change: minimal
Rating: moderate to very difficult
Challenges: bugs, mud, river crossings, logjams, trail finding
Attractions: Ice Lake, Wolf Lake, Gibbon River, fishing, Arctic Grayling, rainbow trout, moose, sandhill cranes, herons, camping
Trailhead: on Norris - Canyon Road, .25 miles (.4 km) west of Canyon Village, at the pullout on the north side of the road
Coordinates: 44.735285, -110.503448

Cascade Lake

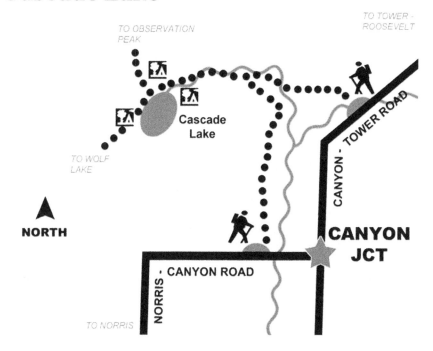

- Fat Ass Friendly - Multi-Mile Trail
- Activity - Camping

Amble over creeks, through meadows, and into forests on a moderately easy 4.2-mile (6.8 km) or 5.2-mile (8.4 km) roundtrip stroll to peaceful Cascade Lake. Cascade Lake, accessible by two trailheads, offers a leisurely first look into Yellowstone's scenic backcountry.

BEFORE YOU GO: **CAMPING PERMITS.** Overnighters in Yellowstone's backcountry must have a Backcountry Use Permit. Campsite reservations may be made in advance. Canyon Visitor Education Center is the closest permitting office to Cascade Lake's trailheads. Call 307-344-2160 or 307-344-7381 for more information.

TRAIL NOTE: **BUGS 'N' MUD!** Wet river areas and lakeshores attract biting mosquitoes. Arm yourself with insect repellant, and use footwear capable of handling muddy conditions!

VIA CASCADE LAKE PICNIC AREA: Find the trailhead at Cascade Lake Picnic Area 1.5 miles (2.4 km) north of Canyon Junction, on Tower - Canyon Road. Follow the trail alongside and across several Cascade Creek rivulets. Gently descend through forests and meadows, enjoying the early summer wildflowers that blanket this valley. Bear right (west) at the trail junction. (The trail to the left leads south to Norris - Canyon Road.) In 2.1 miles (3.4 km) arrive at Cascade Lake. Explore the lake's lovely shores, and return to the trailhead by the same route.

VIA CASCADE CREEK: Find Howard Eaton - Cascade Creek trailhead on the north side of Norris - Canyon Road, less than a half mile (.8 km) west of Canyon Village. Follow the trail for 1.7 miles (2.7 km) along Cascade Creek. Keep an eye out for the moose, bears, and elk that frequent the channel. At Cascade Creek Trail junction, bear left (west) to Cascade Lake. (The trail to the right leads east to Cascade Lake Picnic Area.) In .9 miles (1.5 km) arrive at sparkling Cascade Lake. Relax on the pristine lakeshore, and return to the trailhead by the same route.

CONTINUE THE ADVENTURE: At Cascade Lake, the trail branches north (right) and climbs up steep switchbacks to Observation Peak. The trail to the southwest continues along Howard Eaton Trail to Grebe Lake, Wolf Lake, Ice Lake, and Norris Campground. (See **26. Howard Eaton to... Norris Campground**.)

Length: 4.2 miles (6.8 km) to 5.5 miles (8.9 km) - roundtrip

Estimated time: 3 to 4 hours

Elevation change: less than 100 feet (31 m)

Rating: moderately easy

Challenges: mud, bugs

Attractions: Cascade Lake, Cascade Creek, bears, elk, moose, wildflowers, camping

Trailheads: VIA CASCADE LAKE PICNIC AREA - on the west side of Tower - Canyon Road, 1.5 miles (2.4 km) north of Canyon Junction, at Cascade Lake Picnic Area (44.751629, -110.486013)

VIA CASCADE CREEK - on Norris - Canyon Road, at the pullout on the north side of the road, less than .5 miles (.8 km) west of Canyon Junction (44.735285, -110.503448)

28. North Rim of the Grand Canyon of the Yellowstone River - to Brink of the Upper Falls

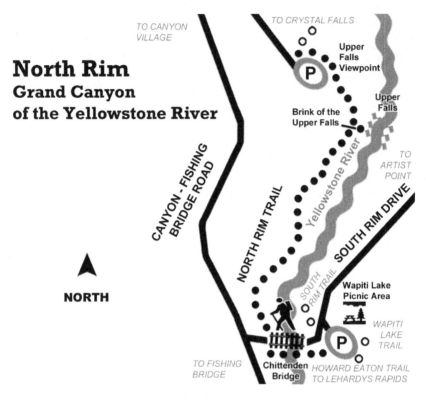

- Fat Ass Friendly
- Attraction - Brink of the Upper Falls
- Self-Guided Trail

Cross historic bridges, following the North Rim of the Grand Canyon of the Yellowstone River to the dramatic brink of the Upper Falls, just like tourists did in the 1800s, on an easy 1.5-mile (2.4 km) out-and-back walk. A level path with outstanding views continues to make North Rim Trail a popular stroll for park visitors throughout the ages.

Find North Rim trailhead 2.3 miles (3.7 km) south of Canyon Junction, east of Canyon - Fishing Bridge Road, across Chittenden Bridge, on the east side of South Rim Drive (Artist Point Drive) at Wapiti Lake Picnic Area. Look for North Rim trailhead on the southwest side of the parking area. Follow paved North Rim Trail west down South Rim Drive (Artist Point Road), and cross the Yellowstone River by way of Chittenden Memorial Bridge.

FIELD NOTE: **EARLY ENGINEERING.** Chittenden Memorial Bridge was named for Captain Hiram Chittenden, an engineer with the Army Corps of Engineers, who constructed the first bridge across the Grand Canyon of the Yellowstone River in 1903. Chittenden's original bridge spanned 120 feet (37 m) across the Yellowstone River and carried visitors and vehicles over the canyon's two rims until 1962 when the new bridge was constructed.

At the end of Chittenden Bridge, cross Artist Point Road and pick up North Rim Trail to the right (north) of the bridge. Follow the trail, which was once an old stagecoach route, north along the western rim of the canyon. Behold the force of the Yellowstone River as it rushes downstream, eroding the rock bed and building the canyon's walls.

Continue on the trail as it crosses historic Canyon Bridge, which spans a usually dry creek bed. Canyon Bridge, completed in 1894 and rebuilt in 1915, ferried tourist-stuffed coaches and automobiles along this major park thoroughfare until Canyon Village roads were realigned in the late 1950s. Today, Canyon Bridge stands as a beautiful, practical footbridge and a tribute to a bygone era.

A few skips beyond the bridge, reach the Brink of the Upper Falls, about .7 miles (1.1 km) from the trailhead. A staircase to the right of the trail leads down to a platform overlooking Upper Falls' jaw-dropping brink. Here, the canyon walls squeeze together and turn the Yellowstone River into a tremendous surge of fast-moving water. At peak spring snowmelt, upwards of 63,000 gallons (238,481 liters) of water gush over the falls every second!

FIELD NOTE: **FORMING THE FALLS.** 640,000 years ago, a massive volcanic eruption in Yellowstone covered the Canyon area in lava flows and ash rocks. Over time, lava and ash turned into mounds of hard rhyolite. Hydrothermal water and gases weakened the rhyolite, allowing the rushing Yellowstone River to erode it away. Upper Falls, at a spectacular 109 feet (33 m), was formed by such erosion on increasingly soft rock beds.

After getting your fill of the falls, walk back up the staircase, and continue north on the trail about 100 yards (91 m) to Upper Falls Viewpoint for another look at the intense gusher. The hike ends here. Retrace your steps back to Wapiti Lake Picnic Area.

CONTINUE THE ADVENTURE: Beyond Upper Falls Viewpoint, North Rim Trail descends 160 feet (49 m) to Crystal Falls and climbs to the Brink of the Lower Falls, with a 600-foot (183 m) descent on a spur path to the brink. The trail ultimately ascends 280 feet (85 m) to Lookout Point, Grandview Point, and Inspiration Point.

Length: 1.5 miles (2.4 km) - roundtrip
Estimated time: 45 minutes
Elevation change: minimal
Rating: easy
Challenge: vertigo views
Attractions: Grand Canyon of the Yellowstone River, Yellowstone River, Brink of the Upper Falls, Chittenden Bridge, Canyon Bridge, self-guided trail
Trailhead: on the east side of South Rim Drive (Artist Point Road) at Wapiti Lake Picnic Area, 2.3 miles (3.7 km) south of Canyon Junction, east of Canyon - Fishing Bridge Road, across Chittenden Bridge
Coordinates: 44.708291, -110.500974

29. South Rim of the Grand Canyon of the Yellowstone River - Artist Point to Point Sublime

South Rim
Grand Canyon
of the Yellowstone River

- Fat Ass Friendly - to Artist Point
- Attractions - Artist Point and Point Sublime
- Self-Guided Trail

Break out the camera! This one's going online! Pick up where spectacular South Rim Drive leaves off in this 4.4-mile (7.1 km) out-and-back hike to Point Sublime.

Find the trailhead at the east end of Artist Point parking area, at the northeast end of South Rim Drive (Artist Point Road), east of Canyon - Fishing Bridge Road and south of Canyon Junction. Follow a level, much-traveled, and often busy paved path to Artist Point overlook, where a scene straight out of a picture book awaits. Against a quintessential western backdrop, the deep blue Yellowstone River spills over majestic 308-foot (94 m) Lower Falls, emerging through the mist and tumbling downstream as it etches through stunning yellow-rose canyon walls topped with pristine pines. It really is a scene just begging to be captured in film!

FIELD NOTE: **ARTISTIC INSPIRATION.** It's easy to see how one's inner artist can be inspired by such fantastic canyon panoramas and waterfall views. Interestingly, this is not the spot where Thomas Moran sketched his renowned 1872 canyon painting. Moran made his sketches from a promontory on the North Rim now known as Moran Point.

Continue east on the path as it transitions to a dirt trail packed with loose and occasionally slippery stones, and enter Yellowstone's backcountry. Heed a sign warning of difficult footing and wilder wildlife, and trek carefully through this region of the canyon.

Travel a half mile (.8 km) along the canyon's rim, past thousand-foot drops and untouched forests, and revel in breath-stealing canyon views. At Ribbon Lake Trail junction, bear left towards Point Sublime. (The trail to the right heads south to Ribbon Lake and deeper into Yellowstone's backcountry.) Hike another .7 miles (1.1 km), and arrive at Point Sublime for another visual feast of canyon scenery. Return to the trailhead by the same route.

Length: 4.4 miles (7.1 km) - roundtrip
Estimated time: 2 to 3 hours
Elevation change: 150 feet (46 m)
Rating: very easy to moderate
Challenges: loose footing, steep drops, vertigo views
Attractions: Grand Canyon of the Yellowstone River, Lower Falls, Artist Point, Point Sublime, self-guided trail
Trailhead: at the east end of Artist Point parking area, at the northeast end of South Rim Drive (Artist Point Drive), east of Canyon - Fishing Bridge Road, south of Canyon Junction
Coordinates: 44.720191, -110.479752

Grand Canyon of the Yellowstone River
© Andrea Hornackova - Dreamstime.com

30. Canyon Lakes Loop - Ribbon Lake, Clear Lake, and Lily Pad Lake

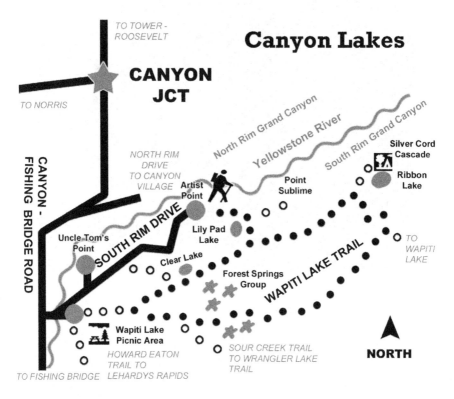

- Attractions - Artist Point and Silver Cord Cascade
- Activity - Camping
- Bear Area

Devour unbelievable views, and indulge in the steaming, bubbling heart of Yellowstone backcountry, on a moderately difficult 7-mile (11.3 km) hike among the unique lakes of the Grand Canyon of the Yellowstone River. Backcountry campsites on Ribbon Lake provide respite for adventurers interested in extended area exploration.

BEFORE YOU GO: **CAMPING PERMITS.** Overnighters in Yellowstone's backcountry must have a Backcountry Use Permit. Campsite reservations may be made in advance. Canyon Visitor Education Center is the closest permitting office to Canyon Lakes' trailheads. Call 307-344-2160 or 307-344-7381 for more information.

TRAIL NOTE: **PREPARE FOR BEARS!** This trail enters a key bear habitat and may be periodically closed due to bear activity. Check current trail accessibility at any visitor center. Use prudence, practice bear safety, and carry bear pepper spray when hiking this trail!

* On July 6, 2011, a hiker was mauled to death by a bear on a trail here after a surprise encounter with a mother grizzly and her cubs. (See **DANGEROUSLY TRUE: TERROR ON WAPITI LAKE TRAIL**.)

TRAIL NOTE: **TOO HOT TO TROT!** Stay on trails in hydrothermal areas to prevent injury to yourself and avoid damage to the environment! Solid-looking ground may really be thin crusts hiding very hot water capable of causing third-degree burns and even death. Constantly changing landscapes make off-trail travel extremely dangerous!

Find the trailhead at the east end of Artist Point parking area, at the northeast end of South Rim Drive (Artist Point Drive), just south of Canyon Junction. Follow the paved trail east along the South Rim of the Grand Canyon of the Yellowstone River. Marvel at the striking landscape, as the royal-blue Yellowstone River transforms into dramatic, misty waterfalls, rushing through towering golden canyon walls.

Continue east and pick up a dirt path heading into Yellowstone's backcountry. Take extra caution in this area of slippery footing and dangerous drop-offs. Hike through pristine forests, and about .6 miles (1 km) from the trailhead arrive at a trail junction. Bear right (south) to Lily Pad Lake and Ribbon Lake Trail. (The trail to the left heads east to Point Sublime. See **29. South Rim of the Grand Canyon of the Yellowstone River**.) Follow the trail past small Lily Pad Lake, which is naturally sprinkled by lily pads. In .3 miles (.5 km) approach Ribbon Lake Trail junction. Bear left (east) on Ribbon Lake Trail to begin a clockwise loop around Ribbon Lake and Clear Lake. (The trail to the right heads directly to Clear Lake.)

Hike through forests, meadows, and marshes, keeping a keen eye out for bears and big game. Follow Ribbon Lake Trail for about a mile (1.6 km), and arrive near the eastern shores of Ribbon Lake. A short spur trail to the left (east) leads adventurers to the lake's backcountry campsites and a view of 1,200-foot (366 m) Silver Cord Cascade, the tallest waterfall in Wyoming.

From Ribbon Lake Trail bear right (south) and connect with Wapiti Lake Trail. Hike through towering pine forests for about a mile (1.6 km). Cross a small stream and bear right (west) to follow Wapiti Lake Trail past a small pond and meadow.

Leave the pines behind and follow the path for 2 miles (3.2 km), gradually descending through an open plain. Watch for bison grazing in the grasses. Pass through alien-like Forest Springs Group, a geothermal colony of mudpots, rainbow pools, and reeking sulfur vents. These features are more noticeable off-trail and slightly to the north as they crack through the ghostly white terrain.

Arrive at Sour Creek Trail junction, and bear right (west) to stay on Wapiti Lake Trail. Trek through forests and meadows. Approach another intersection in .3 miles (.5 km), and turn right (east) towards Clear Lake and Ribbon Lake. (The trail to the left leads west to Upper Falls and the highway.)

Hike along this trail for less than a half mile (.8 km). At the next trail junction, bear right towards Clear Lake. (The trail to the left heads northwest to South Rim Drive and Lower Falls.)

Pass the southern shores Clear Lake, a large sizzling green pool. Continue east, navigating through the northern periphery of Forest Springs Group and enduring the pungent odor of rotten feet. In .8 miles (1.3 km) close the trail loop by bearing left at the trail junction towards Lily Pad Lake. Bear left at South Rim Trail to return to Artist Point and the parking lot.

Length: 7 miles (11.3 km) - roundtrip
Estimated time: 3 to 4 hours
Elevation change: about 300 feet (91 m)
Rating: moderately difficult
Challenges: bears, slippery footing, steep drop-offs, vertigo views
Attractions: Artist Point, Silver Cord Cascade, Lily Pad Lake, Ribbon Lake, Clear Lake, Forest Springs, bears, buffalo, camping
Trailhead: at the east end of Artist Point parking area, at the northeast end of South Rim Drive (Artist Point Drive), just south of Canyon Junction
Coordinates: 44.720191, -110.479752

FORGET IT, FAT ASS Hikes In This Area:

- ## Observation Peak

A high-elevation hike up to the top of 9,397-foot (2,864 m) Observation Peak, this sweat-maker offers an outstanding view of the Yellowstone wilderness, a 1,400-ft (427 m) climb over 3 miles (4.8 km), and snow cover until summer.

- ## Seven Mile Hole

Seven Mile Hole drops hikers 1,000 feet (305 m) to the bottom of the Grand Canyon of the Yellowstone River and back up again on an 11-mile (17.7 km) roundtrip hike of careful footwork and sharp vigilance past unpredictable geothermal features.

- ## Uncle Tom's Trail

Uncle Tom's Trail has been whipping tourists' butts since 1898 when purveyor "Uncle Tom" Richardson used rope ladders to lead tours down to the bottom of power gusher Lower Falls and the Grand Canyon of the Yellowstone River. Although a series of 300 steel stairs helps modern-day hikers cruise down 500 feet (152 m) three-quarters of the way into the canyon to Lower Falls, the return hike back up those 300 steps is brutal. Luckily, there are plenty of other places along the South Rim to enjoy canyon scenery and waterfall views.

- ## Brink of the Lower Falls

Spectacular as it may be to stand on the cusp of tremendous Lower Falls, the tallest waterfall near a road in Yellowstone at 308 feet (94 m) (much taller than Niagara Falls), and view the torrential 63,500 gallons (240,373 liters) of water per second that gush over the brink at peak runoff, this strenuous one-mile (1.6 km) out-and-back trail to the falls shuttles hikers a breath-snatching 600 feet (183 m) in a half mile (.8 km) down steep switchbacks into the canyon to the viewing platform.

• Mary Mountain

A fading foot trail soars 1,100 (335 m) up 8,573-foot (2,613 m) flat-topped Mary Mountain, which overlooks the bison and grizzly stomping grounds of the Hayden Valley and the Central Plateau. Active grizzlies make traversing this trail extremely unadvisable for solo hikers. From Mary Mountain, the trail ambles down to Mary Lake and Nez Perce Creek to end 21 miles (33.8 km) later clear on the other side of Grand Loop Road.

DANGEROUSLY TRUE:

MARY MOUNTAIN MAULING

In August of 2001, a man from Michigan was fatally mauled by a grizzly bear on Mary Mountain Trail. The man had been hiking alone, possibly by a grizzly-attracting bison carcass. The grizzly culprit was found... after it had been linked by DNA analysis to the death of another hiker in the Canyon area. (See **DANGEROUSLY TRUE: TERROR ON WAPITI LAKE TRAIL**.) *The grizzly was ultimately euthanized.*

Old Faithful Area

ROAD NOTE: Roads into the Old Faithful area are closed from roughly mid-fall to mid-spring.

Old Faithful Area Highlights:

- Old Faithful Geyser
- Grand Prismatic Spring
- Geothermal Features
- Nez Perce Trail
- Waterfalls

FAT ASS FRIENDLY Hikes In This Area:
(trail number and name)

31. Nez Perce Creek - to Cowan Creek
33. Lower Geyser Basin - Fountain Paint Pot ++
34. Midway Geyser Basin - Grand Prismatic Spring +
35. Fairy Falls
36. Biscuit Basin +
37. Mystic Falls
38. Black Sand Basin +
39. Old Faithful Loop +
41. Geyser Hill
42. Upper Geyser Basin +
44. Lone Star Geyser

+ wheelchair and stroller accessible
++ wheelchair and stroller accessible - with assistance

NOTE: Wheelchair rental is available at Old Faithful Medical Clinic.

Information:

Park Information - 307-344-7381

- Old Faithful Visitor Education Center

Old Faithful Visitor Education Center is located in Old Faithful Village. Its exhibits highlight Yellowstone's hydrothermal features.

- Old Faithful Ranger Station

Old Faithful Ranger Station is located in Old Faithful Village, southwest of the Visitor Education Center. The ranger station also houses a backcountry office.

Medical Services:

Medcor operates a medical clinic offering urgent care services in Old Faithful Village during the summer season. Hours may vary.

Clinic information - 307-344-7325

Eats:

SUMMER OPTIONS
- Old Faithful Inn Dining Room
- Old Faithful Lodge Cafeteria
- Old Faithful Lodge Snack Shop (fast food)
- Snow Lodge Restaurant
- Snow Lodge Geyser Grill (fast food)
- Old Faithful Lower General Store (groceries, restaurant)
- Old Faithful Upper General Store (groceries, restaurant)
- Old Faithful Basin Store (fast food)
- Old Faithful Photo Shop (fast food)
- Old Faithful BAC Store (fast food)
- Four Seasons Snack Shop (fast food)
- Pony Express Snack Shop (fast food)

WINTER OPTIONS

- Snow Lodge Dining Room
- Snow Lodge Geyser Grill (fast food)

long*THE HIKES:*

31. Nez Perce Creek

Nez Perce Creek

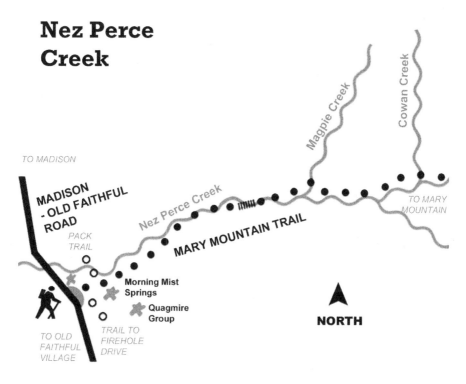

- Fat Ass Friendly - to footbridge, Multi-Mile Trail
- Attraction - Nez Perce Historic Trail

Hike history along the Nez Perce National Historic Trail, the same path traveled in 1877 by Nez Perce reservation resisters fleeing the US Army. Explore the majesty of this ancient pathway of both man and beast, following one of America's great bison migration routes through vast meadows, up Nez Perce Creek, and across Yellowstone's Central Plateau. This relatively flat journey along Mary Mountain Trail is rated moderately easy to very difficult due to its 14-mile (22.5 km) there-and-back length. Significant wildlife habitats prevent convenient camping options, so Nez Perce must be tackled as a day hike. Fortunately, an easy walk to the footbridge makes a lovely and relaxed 4-mile (6.4 km) roundtrip jaunt.

TRAIL NOTE: **PREPARE FOR BEARS!** This trail enters a key bear habitat and is closed from Nez Perce trailhead to Mary Lake from mid-March to mid-June. Use prudence, practice bear safety, and carry bear pepper spray when hiking this trail!

TRAIL NOTE: **MARSH MADNESS!** Nez Perce Creek's meadows and banks may be soggy in spring and early summer, so wear appropriate marsh-mucking shoes on this hike. Wet river areas also attract biting mosquitoes. Arm yourself with insect repellant!

Find Nez Perce Creek - Mary Mountain trailhead 6.5 miles (10.5 km) south of Madison Junction and 9.3 miles (15 km) north of Old Faithful Junction, on the east side of Madison - Old Faithful Road. Follow the trail northeast as it leaves the western edge of Fountain Flats in the Lower Geyser Basin and enters a meadow. Pass Porcupine Hills and continue straight (east) at the trail intersection. Skirt the edge of hydrothermal Morning Mist Springs on the left (north) side of the trail.

Keep an eye out for bison along this hike as grassy meadows and percolating hot springs create a frolicking buffalo heaven. This route through the Central Plateau follows one of America's major native bison migration routes.

Follow Culex Basin along Nez Perce Creek, a tributary of the Firehole River jumping with trout and quite attractive to bears. Cross a small stream, and watch for colorful springs bubbling along the banks of the Nez Perce. Remember to tread carefully in unrestricted thermal areas as the ground may only faintly cover hot water hazards.

About 2.5 miles (4 km) from the trailhead, cross Nez Perce Creek by means of a small wooden footbridge, and follow the northern banks of the creek east. Meander through a beautiful meadow as the trail opens up to Yellowstone's vast Central Plateau.

FIELD NOTE: **FLIGHT OF THE NEZ PERCE.** Nez Perce Creek follows a trail walked for thousands of years by countless generations of Native Americans. In the summer of

1877, more than 800 Nez Perce resisting forced resettlement on reservations fled the advancing US Army by crossing through Yellowstone. The Nez Perce were hoping to reach the safety of Canada but were ultimately stopped in a crushing fight just shy of the border. Their path is honored as the sacred Nez Perce National Historic Trail.

Continue on the trail as it winds through stands of lodgepole pines. A little over 5 miles (8.1 km) from the trailhead, bend across the banks of Magpie Creek. Follow Nez Perce Trail through another sweeping meadow that climbs northeast towards 8,573-foot (2,613 m) Mary Mountain.

FIELD NOTE: **BATTLE OF THE WOLVES.** In addition to following a major bison migration route, Nez Perce Creek also anchored the Nez Perce wolf pack. In 2006 the Nez Perce pack was finally decimated by the Gibbon Meadows pack, which expanded their territory into these bison-rich lands.

About 7.25 miles (11.7 km) from the trailhead, reach Cowan Creek. Cowan Creek is the site of one of the few Yellowstone conflicts during the Flight of the Nez Perce.

FIELD NOTE: **CAPTURED!** In August of 1877, George and Emma Cowan camped with a sightseeing party along Cowan Creek. Nez Perce, trying to evade the US Army, came upon the tourists. George Cowan sassed the Nez Perce when the band tried to commandeer the party's supplies. He was shot and the Nez Perce held the rest of the party hostage for a few hours before releasing them.

The hike ends here. Retrace your steps back to the trailhead. [The trail beyond Cowan Creek leads up to 20-acre (8 hectare) Mary Lake, to Mary Mountain, and onto Canyon Village - Fishing Bridge Road.]

Length: 14.5 miles (23.3 km) - roundtrip
Estimated time: 5 to 8 hours
Elevation change: minimal
Rating: moderately easy to very difficult
Challenges: bears, bugs, marshy areas, hydrothermal area
Attractions: Nez Perce Historical Route, Nez Perce Creek, bears, bison, Mary Mountain
Trailhead: at the turnout on the east side of Madison - Old Faithful Road, 6.5 miles (10.5 km) south of Madison Junction and 9.3 miles (15 km) north of Old Faithful Junction
Coordinates: 44.569915, -110.816134

32. Sentinel Meadows - Queen's Laundry

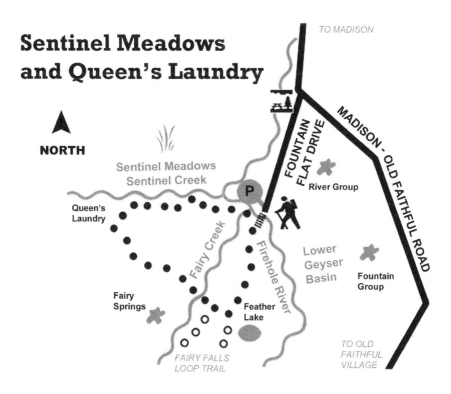

Sentinel Meadows and Queen's Laundry

- Attraction - Queen's Laundry National Historic Site

Grasses bubbling with hot springs lead adventurers to a fascinating National Historic Site on this moderate 4-mile (6.4 km) roundtrip hike through Sentinel Meadows to Queen's Laundry bathhouse.

TRAIL NOTE: **BUGS 'N' MUD!** Wet river areas attract biting mosquitoes, especially in spring. Arm yourself with insect repellant, and use footwear capable of handling muddy conditions!

TRAIL NOTE: **TOO HOT TO TROT!** Stay on trails in hydrothermal areas to prevent injury to yourself and avoid damage to the environment! Solid-looking ground may really be thin crusts hiding very hot water capable of causing third-degree burns and even death. Constantly changing landscapes make off-trail travel extremely dangerous!

Find the trailhead 10 miles (16.1 km) north of Old Faithful Village, off of Old Faithful - Madison Road, on Fountain Flat Drive. Drive southwest down Fountain Flat Drive, pass the picnic area, and park in the area on the right (west) side of the road before the steel footbridge.

Follow the trail as it crosses the Firehole River by way of a footbridge. Bear right (northwest) at the trail loop, and head for Sentinel Meadows. (The trail to the left heads south to Feather Lake.) Hike along the Firehole River, and cross Fairy Creek. Follow the path as it bends west along the southern banks of Sentinel Creek. Enter soggy meadows sweating from scalding springs and bulging with large, crusty hot spring cones capped with steaming pools.

Reach the heart of Sentinel Meadows 1.6 miles (2.6 km) from the trailhead. Take note of fragile terraces created by spring-deposited sinter. The large hot spring framed by sinter terraces at the western edge of the meadow is Red Terrace Spring. Look across Red Terrace for the remnants of a log cabin submerged in the steaming water. This is Queen's Laundry bathhouse.

FIELD NOTE: **HISTORIC HALF BATH.** Queen's Laundry is a National Historic Site. Built in 1881 as a bathhouse for tourists, it is the oldest national park structure constructed by the government for visitors. Queen's Laundry was never completed and remains uniquely preserved by the hot spring's minerals.

From Queen's Laundry, retrace your steps back to the trailhead.

ALTERNATE RETURN: Follow the trail southeast as it loops through forests and meadows over Fairy Creek. Bear left at the Fairy Falls Trail loops, and head north away from Feather Lake back to Fountain Flat Drive and the trailhead.

Length: 4 miles (6.4 km) - roundtrip
Estimated time: 1.5 to 2 hours
Elevation change: minimal
Rating: moderate
Challenges: marshy areas, bugs, hydrothermal area
Attractions: Queen's Laundry National Historic Site, Sentinel Meadows, hot springs
Trailhead: 10 miles (16.1 km) north of Old Faithful Village, off of Old Faithful - Madison Road, on Fountain Flat Drive; drive southwest down Fountain Flat Drive, pass the picnic area, and park in the area on the right (west) side of the road before the steel footbridge
Coordinates: 44.56216, -110.838686

33. Lower Geyser Basin - Fountain Paint Pot

- Fat Ass Friendly
- Wheelchair and Stroller Accessible - with assistance
- Attraction - Fountain Paint Pot
- Self-Guided Trail

Get to know Yellowstone's different types of hydrothermal features on this very easy short-and-sweet half-mile (.8 km) boardwalk stroll among the geysers, hot springs, fumaroles, and mudpots of the Lower Geyser Basin.

TRAIL NOTE: **TOO HOT TO TROT!** Stay on boardwalks in hydrothermal areas to prevent injury to yourself and avoid damage to the environment! Solid-looking ground may really be thin crusts hiding very hot water capable of causing third-degree burns and even death. Constantly changing landscapes make off-trail travel extremely dangerous!

Find the Fountain Paint Pot boardwalk 8 miles (12.9 km)

north of Old Faithful, on the west side of Madison - Old Faithful Road. Follow the boardwalk north to Celestine Pool, a steaming spring as bright blue as the heavens above. Across the path to the right, notice prismatic bacterial mats thriving in the geyser basin's thermal runoff. Here, each color of microorganism needs a different temperature of water to survive.

At the loop junction, bear right for a counterclockwise tour of Fountain Paint Pot Nature Trail and the most direct access to the basin's stunners. First up is Silex Spring, a piping hot spring awash in complementary aqua and red hues. Silex is another name for silica.

As the trail crooks left, see the main attraction - Fountain Paint Pot, a steaming, bubbling crater. This colorful churning mudpot is named for its likeness to a paint can. The painterly reds and yellows are due to oxidizing iron in the mud. Mudpots form when microorganisms convert gasses to hydrogen sulfide, which breaks down solid rock to clay. The muddy bubbling is due to escaping gasses.

Bear right as the boardwalks loops around Leather Pool, a rugged-looking hot pool covered with brown hot water-loving bacteria. The former Fountain Hotel once used these waters to supply their hot baths. Across from Leather Pool is Red Spouter, a result of the violent 1959 Hebgen Lake Earthquake.

FIELD NOTE: **CHANGING FEATURES.** Red Spouter, named for the ruddy water it sometimes churns and splashes about in its crater, is an excellent example of the sensitive nature of hydrothermal features. Red Spouter may take the form of any of Yellowstone's four hydrothermal features, depending on the condition of basin's water table. In the wet months of spring and early summer, Red Spouter is a bubbling mud pit. In the dry months of late summer and fall, it is a wheezing vent, expelling steamy gasses.

Head west to Twig Geyser, a small, occasional spurter. Across the path, note the much more impressive Jet Geyser. When active, Jet Geyser roars and hurls out 20-foot (6 m) water-and-steam blasts every few minutes. Next up is Fountain Geyser, a placid blue pool that may suddenly erupt into spectacular 50-foot (15 m) splays. Nearby Morning Geyser rarely blows, but when it does it delivers jaw-dropping eruptions up to 200 feet (61 m). To the west of Morning Geyser is Clepsydra Geyser, which in Greek means water clock. An upshot of the 1959 Hebgen Lake Earthquake, Clepsydra is known for its clockwork discharges and currently erupts almost constantly. Spasm Geyser, also in this active group, is minor by comparison with small sprays only a few feet high.

Follow the boardwalk as it travels south. On the west side of the trail notice sinter deposited by hot springs. Bear left on the path and travel through a cluster of lodgepole pines. Arrive back at Celestine Pool to complete the loop. Bear right to return to the trailhead.

CONTINUE THE ADVENTURE: **FIREHOLE LAKE DRIVE.** Slightly south of Fountain Paint Pot parking area, on the east side of Old Faithful - Madison Road, is Firehole Lake Drive. Firehole Lake Drive provides wonderful access to additional hot features, including Firehole Lake, a massive travertine terraced hot spring; and Great Fountain Geyser, the only geyser outside of the Old Faithful area where rangers post eruption predictions.

Length: .5 miles (.8 km) - roundtrip
Estimated time: 20 minutes
Elevation change: minimal
Rating: very easy
Challenge: hydrothermal area
Attractions: Fountain Paint Pot, hot springs, fumaroles, mudpots, geysers, self-guided trail
Trailhead: 8 miles (12.9 km) north of Old Faithful on the west side of Old Faithful - Madison Road at the Fountain Paint Pot parking area; across the street from the north exit of Firehole Lake Drive
Coordinates: 44.548494, -110.807291

Midway Geyser Basin

- Fat Ass Friendly
- Wheelchair and Stroller Accessible
- Attraction - Grand Prismatic Spring
- Self-Guided Trail

Get up close and personal with some of the most superlative features in Yellowstone in this very easy half-mile (.8 km) boardwalk loop through compact and colorful Midway Geyser Basin. This short hike takes you along the edge of dazzling rainbow-rimmed Grand Prismatic Spring, one of the largest hot springs in the world.

TRAIL NOTE: **TOO HOT TO TROT!** Stay on boardwalks in hydrothermal areas to prevent injury to yourself and avoid damage to the environment! Solid-looking ground may really be thin crusts hiding very hot water capable of causing third-degree burns and even death. Constantly changing landscapes make off-trail travel extremely dangerous!

FIELD NOTE: **HELL'S HALF ACRE.** In 1889 writer Rudyard Kipling, author of *The Jungle Book*, visited Yellowstone National Park. He called Midway Geyser Basin "Hell's Half Acre" - a fitting name for the infernal area.

True to its name, Midway Geyser Basin is nestled midway between the Upper Geyser Basin and the Lower Geyser Basin. Find the trailhead 6 miles (9.7 km) north of Old Faithful, at the parking area on the west side of Old Faithful - Madison Road. Follow the trail southwest across the Firehole River.

FIELD NOTE: **FIREHOLE HOT AND COLD**. The Firehole River is an interesting mix of cold and hot waters. Grand Prismatic Spring spills about 500 gallons (1,893 liters) of water per minute into the river, while Excelsior Geyser discharges a whopping 4,000 gallons (15,142 liters) of hot water every minute into the river.

Continue on the boardwalk and bear left at the loop junction. Stroll alongside the northern edge of immense Excelsior Geyser Crater, a 200 x 300-foot (61 x 92 m) chasm filled with steaming water. In the 1880s, Excelsior was a very active geyser with violent eruptions reaching as high as 300 feet (91 m). These massive eruptions created its huge crater and monkeyed with its underground plumbing, turning it into a present-day hot spring. Ever unpredictable, Excelsior shot to life for two days in 1985 with constant eruptions before falling silent.

Continue along the boardwalk to the southern periphery of sprawling Grand Prismatic Spring. With a diameter of 200 to 330 feet (61 to 101 m), Grand Prismatic is one of the largest hot springs in the word and is the largest hot spring in the United States. Its prismatic colors are due to thermophiles (heat-loving microorganisms) that thrive in its 160° (71°C) waters. The terraced steps along its edges are created by mineral deposits. Grand Prismatic is about 121 feet (37 m) deep.

* The best way to behold Grand Prismatic's beauty is from above. Fairy Falls Trail (see **35. Fairy Falls**), just south of Midway Geyser Basin, provides cliff-high views of the spring.

Follow the boardwalk past Opal Pool and Turquoise Pool, a pair of shimmering jewel-like hot springs, and complete the loop. Bear left at the junction to return to the trailhead.

Length: .5 miles (.8 km) - roundtrip
Estimated time: 20 minutes
Elevation change: minimal
Rating: very easy
Challenge: hydrothermal area
Attractions: Grand Prismatic Spring, Excelsior Geyser Crater, Firehole River, self-guided trail
Trailhead: 6 miles (9.7 km) north of Old Faithful Village, at the parking area on the west side of Old Faithful - Madison Road
Coordinates: 44.528355, -110.835959

Excelsior Geyser © Geoffrey Kuchera - Dreamstime.com

35. Fairy Falls

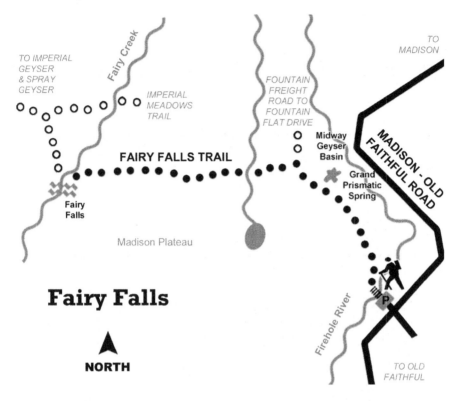

Fairy Falls

▲
NORTH

- Fat Ass Friendly - Multi-Mile Trail
- Attractions - Grand Prismatic Spring, Fairy Falls, Imperial Geyser, and Spray Geyser
- Activity - Bicycling
- Bear Area

Visit enchantment on a moderately easy 5-mile (8.1 km) to 6.4-mile (10.3 km) roundtrip hike to Yellowstone's best water features. This peaceful adventure travels to the edge of awesomely vibrant Grand Prismatic Spring, the largest hot spring in the park, and crests at Fairy Falls, one of the tallest and most dignified waterfalls in Yellowstone.

TRAIL NOTE: **PREPARE FOR BEARS!** This trail enters a key bear habitat and is closed until the Saturday of Memorial Day weekend. Use prudence, practice bear safety, and carry bear pepper spray when hiking this trail!

The shortest way to Fairy Falls is via Old Faithful - Madison Road, where you can find the trailhead 4.5 miles (7.2 km) north of Old Faithful Village, at the parking area on the west side of the road. Follow the trail north across a bridge over the Firehole River. Behind the barricade, continue north on historic Fountain Freight Road, an old wagon route that doubles as a bike path.

Hike along the edge of the Madison Plateau, on the western boundary of the Yellowstone Caldera. Here, just south of Midway Geyser Basin, thermal vapors rise from large hot pools. (See **34. Midway Geyser Basin**.) About .75 miles (1.2 km) from the trailhead, skirt the southern edge of Grand Prismatic Spring.

FIELD NOTE: **GRAND PRISMATIC VIEW.** Climb meandering footpaths up the slopes to the southwest (left) of the trail for an overhead view of gorgeous Grand Prismatic Spring as it shines like a polished slice of agate in a perfect rainbow of hues. Grand Prismatic Spring is Yellowstone's largest and most beautiful hot spring, with a diameter of 200 to 330 feet (61 to 101 m) and a depth of 121 feet (37 m). Its vibrant spectrum of colors are caused by different hydrothermal-loving bacteria.

About a mile (1.6 km) from the trailhead, bear left (west) towards Fairy Falls. (The trail to the right continues north on Fountain Freight Road to Fountain Flat Drive.) Follow Fairy Falls Trail 1.6 miles (2.6 km) through a creepy forest of charred lodgepole pine skeletons, victims of the 1988 Yellowstone wildfires. Notice young pines, aspens, and wild grasses taking root in the carbon-rich soil.

FIELD NOTE: **FIRE DIVERSITY.** Wildfires promote wildlife diversity in Yellowstone and are an integral part of lodgepole pine habitats. Some of the trees' pinecones only open in heat created by intense fires. When opened, the cones release seeds in the nutrient-filled forest floor. New open habitats of lush grasses and regenerating trees crop up, attracting new creatures - and their predators; for example, small mammals feasting on grasses and seeds have brought large birds of prey to the region.

Continue on the trail and cross a cool stream flowing north to

Goose Lake. Pass rich summer wildflowers and enter old growth spruce and Douglas fir stands. These trees prefer the shady conditions that long-standing forests afford. 2.5 miles (4 km) from the trailhead, arrive at the base of dazzling 200-foot (61 m) Fairy Falls, one of the tallest and most beautiful waterfalls in Yellowstone.

In this natural Eden, Fairy Creek elegantly spills over the Madison Plateau, a sprawling lava flow born 600,000 years ago from Yellowstone's last major eruption. Bask in this delightful slice of magnificence, explore Fairy Fall's secret nooks, and return to the trailhead by the same route.

CONTINUE THE ADVENTURE: Tucked another .7 miles (1.1 km) down the trail is beautiful Imperial Geyser and very active Spray Geyser. Simply follow the trail northwest across Fairy Creek, and hike through a meadow. Bear left (west) at Imperial Meadows Trail junction. (The trail to the right heads to the Lower Geyser Basin.) Look to the right (north) of the trail to find thermal neighbors Imperial Geyser and Spray Geyser.

Imperial Geyser is a vaporous blue pool. Named during a park promotion contest in 1927, the once magnificently erupting geyser has since tempered down. Nearby Spray Geyser is a regular eruptor, constantly churning, spurting, and splashing out hot water every few minutes. After enjoying these less-visited geysers, follow your footsteps back to the trailhead.

Length: 5 miles (8.1 km) to Fairy Falls or 6.4 miles (10.3 km) to Imperial Geyser - roundtrip
Estimated time: 3 to 4 hours
Elevation change: minimal
Rating: moderately easy
Challenges: bears, hydrothermal area
Attractions: Fairy Falls, Grand Prismatic Spring, Imperial Geyser, Spray Geyser, bears, bicycling
Trailhead: on Madison - Old Faithful Road, 4.5 miles (7.2 km) north of Old Faithful Village, 1 mile south (1.6 km) of Midway Geyser Basin , at the parking area on the west side of the road
Coordinates: 44.515489, -110.832514

Grand Prismatic Spring © Semnic - Dreamstime.com

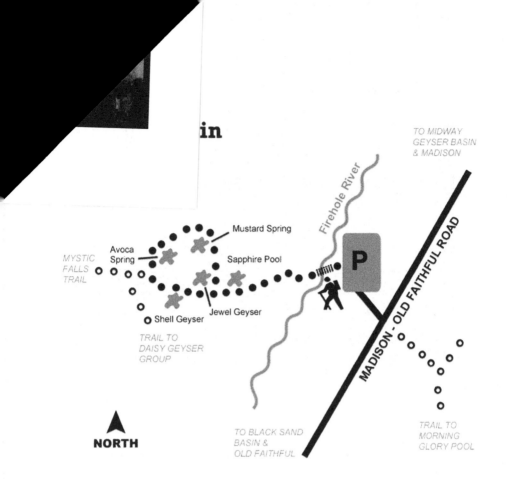

- Fat Ass Friendly
- Wheelchair and Stroller Accessible
- Self-Guided Trail

Get geysered up on this very easy half-mile (.8 km) loop stroll among the beautiful gem-named springs and highly eruptive geysers of volatile Biscuit Basin. Interpretive exhibits along the way illuminate the unusual elements of this thermal hot spot.

TRAIL NOTE: **TOO HOT TO TROT!** Stay on boardwalks in hydrothermal areas to prevent injury to yourself and avoid damage to the environment! Solid-looking ground may really be thin crusts hiding very hot water capable of causing third-degree burns and even death. Constantly changing landscapes make off-trail travel extremely dangerous!

Find the boardwalk trail on Old Faithful - Madison Road, 2

miles (3.2 km) north of Old Faithful Village, at the parking area on the west side of the road. Cross a bridge over the Firehole River, and immediately pass three hot pools - Black Opal Spring, Wall Pool, and Black Diamond Pool - on the right side of the trail. Take a moment to notice the basin's ringed bobbysoxed trees, which are choked by silica from hydrothermal runoff.

Continue down the boardwalk to Sapphire Pool, one of the most beautiful blue pools in Yellowstone. Sapphire Pool is an 18 x 30-foot (6 x 9 m) crater filled with steamy shimmering blue water. Biscuit-shaped deposits that once lined the pool's rim gave Biscuit Basin its name.

FIELD NOTE: **BLOWN UP BISCUITS!** On August 17, 1959, major 7.5 Hebgen Lake Earthquake rumbled through Biscuit Basin. A few days later, Sapphire Pool began to erupt, blowing away the biscuit-shaped formations along its crater. Sapphire Pool doubled in size and became a regularly erupting geyser, shooting out huge 150-foot (46 m) splays for the next few years until falling silent in the late 1960s.

Past Sapphire Pool, the boardwalk forms a loop. Bear left and look to the right to see Jewel Geyser. Pearly sinter deposits around its vent give this geyser its name. Keep your eye on the geyser! Boiling water overflowing from the vent means this baby's about to blow! Jewel Geyser erupts in bursts up to 30 feet (9 m) high every 5 to 10 minutes for about a minute to a minute and a half.

Next up is Shell Geyser. Every 1.5 to 2 hours Shell pushes out spurts averaging 8 feet (2 m) tall. Shell Geyser is named for the warm-toned sinter along its edges, which favors the inside of a mollusk shell.

The boardwalk now intersects with Mystic Falls Trail junction. (See **37. Mystic Falls**.) Bear right on the boardwalk to Avoca Spring. Avoca Spring puts on a show at least every 20 minutes. Watch for telltale signs of the pool churning alive with roiling water. Eruptions last 10 to 30 seconds and reach heights between 10 to 20 feet (3 to 6 m).

Past West Geyser is Mustard Spring, a pair of two yellow-hued springs, each 10 feet (3 m) in diameter and 50 feet (15 m) apart. They are named simply East Mustard Spring and

West Mustard Spring. Constant subterranean changes in Biscuit Basin have consistently affected the activity of both of these geysers. These days, East Mustard Spring is a regularly erupting geyser ejecting 6-foot (2 m) spurts every 10 minutes, while West Mustard is a dry spring.

Continue on the boardwalk and bear left at the loop junction to return to the trailhead.

Length: .5 miles (.8 km) - roundtrip
Estimated time: 30 minutes
Elevation change: minimal
Rating: very easy
Challenge: hydrothermal area
Attractions: Sapphire Pool, Jewel Geyser, erupting geysers, hot springs, Firehole River, self-guided trail
Trailhead: 2 miles (3.2 km) north of Old Faithful Village, on Old Faithful - Madison Road, at the parking area on the west side of the road
Coordinates: 44.485102, -110.852417

Black Opal Spring © Andrea Hornackova - Dreamstime.com

Mystic Falls

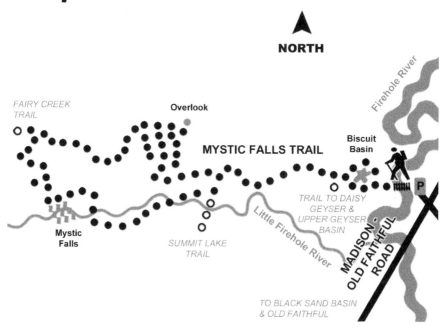

- Fat Ass Friendly - to Mystic Falls, Multi-Mile Trail
- Bear Area

Follow the Little Firehole River through a forest to steamy Mystic Falls on a popular easy-to-very-difficult 2.4-mile (3.9 km) out-and-back hike. An alternative return route offers striking views of Old Faithful and the Upper Geyser Basin.

TRAIL NOTE: **PREPARE FOR BEARS!** This trail enters a key bear habitat and is closed until the Saturday of Memorial Day weekend. Use prudence, practice bear safety, and carry bear pepper spray when hiking this trail!

Find the trailhead 2 miles (3.2 km) north of Old Faithful Village, on the west side of Old Faithful - Madison Road, at the back of the Biscuit Basin boardwalk. (See **36. Biscuit Basin**.) From the parking area, cross the Firehole River via a footbridge, and follow Biscuit Basin boardwalk around a small cluster of hot pools and springs. At the back of the boardwalk by Avoca Spring, meet Mystic Falls Trail.

Follow Mystic Falls Trail west away from the boardwalk, and hike past fallen lodgepole pines, casualties of the 1988 Yellowstone wildfires. In .3 miles (.5 km) arrive at Mystic Falls Loop - Summit Lake Trail junction. Bear left to Mystic Falls. (The trail to the right heads for Biscuit Basin Overlook.)

Bear right (west) at the Summit Lake Trail split to stay on Mystic Falls Loop. Cross the ever-churning Little Firehole River, and arrive at Mystic Falls.

At Mystic Falls, the Little Firehole River drops 70 feet (21 m) over the Madison Plateau to create a unique cascade. Hot, steamy geothermal waters percolating around the falls give it its uniquely mystical aura. A few short and steep spur paths lead south to the base of the falls. Watch your footing in this thermal-laden area!

If you'd like, hike up steep and rocky switchbacks to the top of Mystic Falls. Pause a moment to bask in the ethereal nature of this cascade. Return to the trailhead by the same route.

CONTINUE THE ADVENTURE: For a loop hike with jaw-dropping views, follow the trail up lava flow switchbacks for another 500 feet (152 m) over a half mile (.8 km) to Fairy Creek Trail junction. Catch your breath and feast your eyes on excellent bird's-eye views of the Little Firehole River and the Old Faithful area.

Bear right (east) at Fairy Creek Trail junction to Biscuit Basin Overlook. Hike through dense lodgepole pine forests, and in a half mile (.8 km) reach the overlook. Behold commanding panoramas of the Upper Geyser Basin, including Biscuit Basin, Black Sand Basin, Old Faithful, and the Firehole River. Time it right and you may just see a few choice geyser eruptions.

Follow the trail .7 miles (1.1 km) back to Mystic Falls Trail loop junction. Bear left (east) to return to Biscuit Basin and the parking area.

Length: 2 miles (3.2 km) - roundtrip

Estimated time: 1 to 3 hours

Elevation change: minimal to 500 feet (152 m)

Rating: easy to very difficult

Challenges: bears, optional 500-foot (152 m) ascent over .5 miles (.8 km)

Attractions: Biscuit Basin, Mystic Falls, Little Firehole River, bears

Trailhead: 2 miles (3.2 km) north of Old Faithful Village on Old Faithful - Madison Road, at the pullout on the west side of the road. Find the trailhead at the back of Biscuit Basin boardwalk, near Avoca Spring.

Coordinates: 44.485102, -110.852417

38. Black Sand Basin

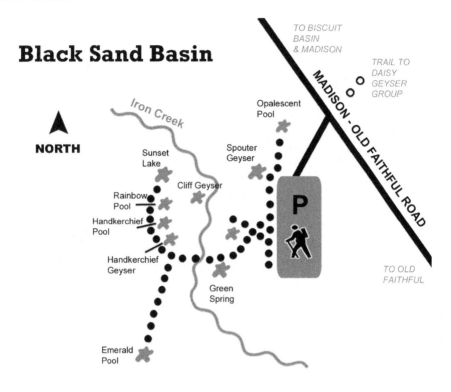

Black Sand Basin

- Fat Ass Friendly
- Wheelchair and Stroller Accessible
- Self-Guided Trail

Romp about a rainbow of color on a very easy half-mile (.8 km) boardwalk tour around small but super chromatic Black Sand Basin.

TRAIL NOTE: **TOO HOT TO TROT!** Stay on boardwalks in hydrothermal areas to prevent injury to yourself and avoid damage to the environment! Solid-looking ground may really be thin crusts hiding very hot water capable of causing third-degree burns and even death. Constantly changing landscapes make off-trail travel extremely dangerous!

FIELD NOTE: **BLACK GLASS SAND.** Black Sand Basin takes its name from fine-grained obsidian sand strewn about the basin. Obsidian is a dark glasslike volcanic rock that is formed when lava rapidly solidifies but does not crystallize.

Find the branching boardwalk at the parking area on the west side of Old Faithful - Madison Road, a half mile (.8 km) north of Old Faithful Village. Follow the left boardwalk over Iron Creek by way of a footbridge. Thermophiles (heat-thriving microorganisms) cause the striking colors of Black Sand Basin. Rust-colored organisms, not iron metal, climbs the banks of Iron Creek to create its florid appearance.

Follow the left branch of the left boardwalk to famous Emerald Pool hot spring. Jewel-green Emerald Pool is a Yellowstone icon. This pool, at 154°F (68°C), is not as hot as other springs in this area. It supports a colony of yellow thermophiles. Blue wavelengths reflected by the pool mix with the yellow colors of the microorganisms to create a luscious emerald-green tone that shimmers from the 27 x 38-foot (8 x 12 m) pool.

Backtrack to the right branch of the left boardwalk to see Handkerchief Geyser and Handkerchief Pool, former stars of the basin. Early park tourists would drop their handkerchiefs into the spring, and the cloths would be sucked away by thermal currents (convection) and later regurgitated, squeaky clean, on the spring's surface. A different era, indeed! Ultimately the effects of human interference took its toll on the spring, and it is now inactive.

Past Handkerchief group is Rainbow Pool. Here, colorfully banded microorganism communities thrive on the pool's edges. Continue on the boardwalk to Sunset Lake, a shallow hot pool about 20 feet (6 m) deep. Super steamy Sunset Lake erupts every once in a while, with splashes only a few feet high. From Sunset Lake backtrack to the parking lot.

The middle boardwalk from the parking lot leads to an observation platform overlooking Iron Creek and Cliff Geyser. Cliff Geyser blows its stack every now and again with gushers up to 40 feet (12 m). Cliff's gushers are precipitated by churning water filling the geyser's crater. Notice the stacks of siliceous deposits around the crater that give the geyser its name.

From the parking lot, follow the right boardwalk to Spouter Geyser. Stay for the show at this fountain-like gusher.

Eruptions are more like major churnings that average 6 feet (2 m) in height. After a good 10-hour eruption, water drains from Spouter's crater and it stays silent for an hour or two before starting up again.

Continue past Spouter Geyser to Opalescent Pool. Once dry, prismatic Opalescent Pool now accommodates Spouter's overflow. Notice stands of dead lodgepole pines deluged by the mineral-rich waters of this pool. The whiteness on the tree trunks is caused by silica deposits which have created a deadly smothering bobbysox effect. Return to the trailhead by the same route.

Length: .5 miles (.8 km) - roundtrip
Estimated time: 30 minutes
Elevation change: minimal
Rating: very easy
Challenge: hydrothermal area
Attractions: Emerald Pool, Iron Creek, geysers, hot pools, self-guided trail
Trailhead: .5 miles (.8 km) north of Old Faithful Village on Old Faithful - Madison Road, at the parking area on the west side of the road
Coordinates: 44.462195, -110.853312

Black Sand Basin © Andrea Hornackova - Dreamstime.com

39. Old Faithful Loop

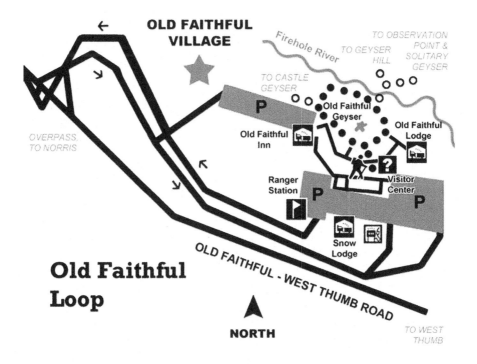

- Fat Ass Friendly
- Wheelchair and Stroller Accessible
- Attraction - Old Faithful Geyser
- Self-Guided Trail

Circle the most famous geyser in the world in a very easy .7-mile (1.1 km) loop around Yellowstone's superstar attraction and showy mainstay, Old Faithful. Break through the tourist circus for 360-degree every-which-way enjoyment of this thermal-rific spectacular.

TRAIL NOTE: **TOO HOT TO TROT!** Stay on boardwalks and trails in hydrothermal areas to prevent injury to yourself and avoid damage to the environment! Solid-looking ground may really be thin crusts hiding very hot water capable of causing third-degree burns and even death. Constantly changing landscapes make off-trail travel extremely dangerous!

Find the boardwalk entrance in the heart of the Old Faithful Historic District, just north of Old Faithful Visitor Center. Follow the path north to the Old Faithful viewing platform. Note the platform is crafted from three million plastic milk jugs. Recycled plastics are a go-to material to replace aging wooden boardwalks that leach toxic chemicals into the environment.

Just beyond the viewing platform is iconic Old Faithful Geyser. This portrait of American repute is the most frequently erupting large geyser in the park, expelling a tremendous gush of boiling 204°F (96°C) water, up to 8,400 gallons (31,797 liters) every 90 minutes or so. These bursts last up to five minutes and can reach heights over 180 feet (55 m). Eruption predictions are posted at the Visitor Center.

FIELD NOTE: **OLD FAITHFUL FACT AND FICTION.** Although Old Faithful was named in 1870 by the Washburn Expedition for its clockwork-like eruptions, it is neither the most predictable nor the largest erupting geyser in Yellowstone. (See **42. Upper Geyser Basin** to visit Grand Geyser, the tallest, most predictable geyser in the world. See **17. Norris Geyser Basin** to visit Steamboat Geyser, Yellowstone's largest eruptor.) Predictions about Old Faithful's eruptions are made by examining the relationship between the eruption durations and the length of the proceeding intervals. Eruption length and height vary day-to-day, and are often influenced by earthquakes, buildup of mineral deposits, and human interference. Old Faithful's eruptions most likely do not signal when Yellowstone's super-volcano is about to blow up. Contrary to urban legend, park rangers do not, and cannot, control Old Faithful's eruptions.

Follow Old Faithful's boardwalk counterclockwise around the geyser. Consider the underground thermal channels that generate Old Faithful's powerful explosions. Hot water fills constricted chambers below the geyser, which are then blocked by rising gas bubbles. Pressure and temperature build in the chambers until steam and water force their way out of the geyser's mouth in a tremendous eruption. The eruption empties the subterranean channels. The channels then refill with hot water to restart the eruption cycle.

Continue on the boardwalk past Old Faithful Lodge. The trail now transitions to a paved path. Head northwest and arrive at a junction. Bear left to continue the loop around Old Faithful. (The trail to the right leads across the Firehole River to **40. Observation Point and Solitary Geyser** and **41. Geyser Hill**.) The trail becomes a boardwalk again as it travels west along the Firehole River. Watch for bison and elk, which are attracted to Old Faithful's cozy hydrothermal areas.

Across the river from Beehive Geyser (part of the Geyser Hill group), the boardwalk again transitions to a paved path, bending south to a trail intersection. Bear left to Old Faithful Inn. (The trail to the right leads to Castle Geyser.)

FIELD NOTE: **CHAOS AND NATURE.** Old Faithful Inn, a National Historic Landmark, was designed by Robert C. Reamer, who used the chaos of nature to influence the building's asymmetrical design. This magnificent log hotel opened in 1904.

Complete Old Faithful loop as the path returns to the Visitor Center.

Length: .7 miles (1.1 km) - roundtrip
Estimated time: 20 minutes
Elevation change: minimal
Rating: very easy
Challenge: hydrothermal area
Attractions: Old Faithful Geyser, bison, elk, Old Faithful Inn, Firehole River, self-guided trail
Trailhead: in Old Faithful Village, just north of Old Faithful Visitor Center, between Old Faithful Inn and Old Faithful Lodge
Coordinates: 44.458991, -110.829076

Old Faithful Crowd © Lizzy Myers

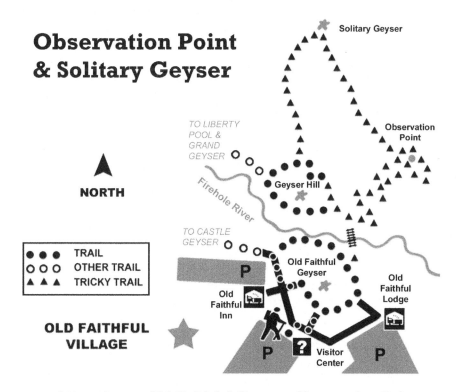

Observation Point & Solitary Geyser

- Attractions - Old Faithful Geyser, Observation Point, and Solitary Geyser

Slip away from the crowds, conquer a difficult 200-foot (61 m) hill, get a rare bird's-eye view of Old Faithful, and visit regularly erupting Solitary Geyser on this 1.8-mile (2.9 km) roundtrip loop hike.

In Old Faithful Village, find Old Faithful Visitor Center and head north through throngs of geyser admirers to the Old Faithful boardwalk. Walk counterclockwise around the boardwalk. In the back northeast corner, find Geyser Hill trailhead. Bear right on the paved trail, and cross the Firehole River by way of a bridge. Watch for elk and bison gamboling in Old Faithful's attractively warm hydrothermal areas.

Arrive at Observation Point Trail junction, and bear right on the dirt trail towards Observation Point. (The trail to the left leads to **41. Geyser Hill** and Solitary Geyser.) Climb switchbacks and cross footbridges as the trail ascends 160 feet (49 m) over a half mile (.8 km) through steep woodlands and marshes. At the top of the hill, bear right to Observation Point overlook, an exposed rhyolite outcropping. (The trail to the left leads to Solitary Geyser.)

Soak up the view at this prime vantage point of Yellowstone's Upper Geyser Basin, home to an astounding 25% of the Earth's geysers. Gaze down on Old Faithful for a unique box-seat view of its much-hailed eruptions. Marvel at steadfast Old Faithful Inn, a National Historic Landmark dating back to 1903, which narrowly escaped the notorious 1988 wildfires that scorched most of this region.

Follow the trail west and bear right at the junctions to Solitary Geyser. (The trails to the left lead back to Old Faithful.) In .3 miles (.5 km) arrive at frequently erupting Solitary Geyser. Solitary Geyser erupts every 4 to 8 minutes with small expulsions of less than 6 feet (2 m).

FIELD NOTE: **TAMPERED!** Solitary Geyser is a testament to the effects of human interference on the natural world. This thermal feature was once known as Solitary Spring, a serene hot pool that did not erupt. Water from Solitary was diverted to fill a swimming pool near Old Faithful Inn. This lowered water levels in the spring, added pressure to its constricted water supply, and triggered eruptions. The diversion of water ended in the 1940s, but Solitary Geyser remains too unstable to revert back to a hot spring.

Continue on the trail as it descends back to the Geyser Hill boardwalk. Bear left at the Geyser Hill loop. (The trail to the right leads to Grand Geyser. See **41. Geyser Hill.**) Stay left at the next intersection to connect back with Observation Point Trail. (The trail to the right is the return loop of Geyser Hill.) Bear right at the trail junction, and cross the Firehole River back to Old Faithful.

Length: 1.8 miles (2.9 km) - roundtrip
Estimated time: 1 to 2 hours
Elevation change: 160 feet (49 m)
Rating: difficult
Challenges: 160-foot (49 m) ascent, hydrothermal area
Attractions: Upper Geyser Basin views, periodically erupting Solitary Geyser, Observation Point, Old Faithful, Firehole River
Trailhead: north of Old Faithful Visitor Center in Old Faithful Village; walk counterclockwise around Old Faithful boardwalk and bear right at Geyser Hill trailhead; cross the Firehole River and find Observation Point trailhead on the right
Coordinates: 44.458991, -110.829076

Old Faithful from Above © Jeffrey Williams - Dreamstime.com

41. Geyser Hill

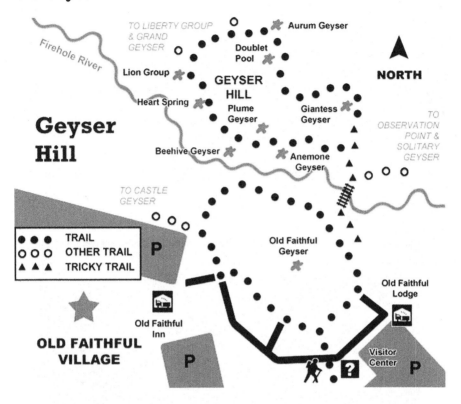

- Fat Ass Friendly
- Self-Guided Trail

Delve deep into geyser country on this short, easy 1.3-mile (2.1 km) boardwalk loop through a wondrous mix of hot spots bubbling behind Old Faithful. Geyser Hill is an incredibly dense region of geothermal attractions, from continuous boilers to rare, enormous exploders.

TRAIL NOTE: **TOO HOT TO TROT!** Stay on boardwalks and trails in hydrothermal areas to prevent injury to yourself and avoid damage to the environment! Solid-looking ground may really be thin crusts hiding very hot water capable of causing third-degree burns and even death. Constantly changing landscapes make off-trail travel extremely dangerous!

From Old Faithful Visitor Center, walk north to Old Faithful boardwalk, following the path counterclockwise to the east and north as it turns to a paved trail. Bear right at Geyser Hill trailhead, and cross the Firehole River by bridge. At the next junction, bear left on the boardwalk to Geyser Hill loop. (The unpaved trail to the right leads to **40. Observation Point - Solitary Geyser**.)

At the loop junction, bear right on the boardwalk to Giantess Geyser. Ferocious Giantess erupts a few times a year in 100- to 200-foot (31 to 61 m) fountain-like bursts which are often preceded by subterranean steam rumblings. Continue on the trail to cobalt-blue Doublet Pool, an occasionally churning network of hot springs ringed by intricate ledges. Next up to the right of the trail is Aurum Geyser. Aurum Geyser regularly erupts every few hours in bursts reaching 25 feet (8 m).

Bear left (west) at the next two trail junctions. (The trails to the right lead to Solitary Geyser and Grand Geyser.) Arrive at Lion Group, a network for four geysers - Lion, Lioness, Big Cub, and Little Cub - which are connected by underground channels. Lion sports the largest cone in the pride. During its daily eruptions, Lion roars as steam and water boom from its jowls.

Continue south on the boardwalk to Heart Spring, a hot pool whose blue chamber is shaped like a human heart. As the trail loops again east, see glorious Beehive Geyser. Beehive explodes twice a day in splays that can reach over 150 feet (46 m). Look to the left of the trail. Here, Plume Geyser shoots out 25-foot (8 m) spurts every 20 minutes. Across the trail to the right, on the banks of the Firehole River, highly active double geyser Anemone roils and pushes out moderate splays every few minutes.

Past Anemone Geyser, Geyser Hill loop closes. Bear right, cross the Firehole River, and follow the Old Faithful boardwalk back to Old Faithful Village.

Length: 1.3 miles (2.1 km) - roundtrip
Estimated time: 45 minutes
Elevation change: minimal
Rating: easy
Challenge: hydrothermal area

Attractions: geysers, self-guided trail
Trailhead: in Old Faithful Village, north of Old Faithful Visitor Center, follow Old Faithful boardwalk counterclockwise to the back northeast corner to Geyser Hill trailhead
Coordinates: 44.458991, -110.829076

Heart Spring © Andrea Hornackova - Dreamstime.com

42. Upper Geyser Basin - to Castle Geyser, Grand Geyser, Giant Geyser, Grotto Geyser, Daisy Geyser, Riverside Geyser, and Morning Glory Pool

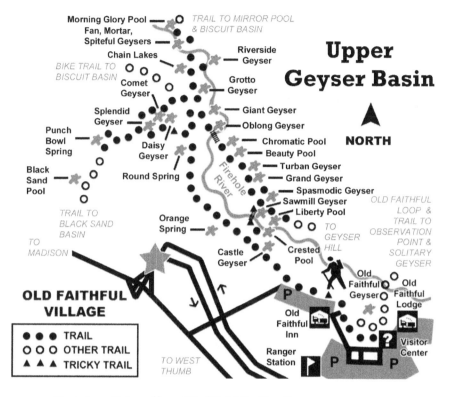

- Fat Ass Friendly - Multi-Mile Trail
- Wheelchair and Stroller Accessible - in parts
- Attractions - Castle Geyser, Grand Geyser, Daisy Geyser, Riverside Geyser, and Morning Glory Pool
- Self-Guided Trail
- Activity - Bicycling

Meander among the largest concentration of geysers in the world on a matrix of easy walkways connecting the first-class hot spots of the Upper Geyser Basin. This out-and-back hike to beauteous Morning Glory Pool (and Biscuit Basin gateway) is 5.6 miles (9 km) roundtrip, with plenty of side loops and many wheelchair-and-stroller-accessible areas.

TRAIL NOTE: **TOO HOT TO TROT!** Stay on boardwalks and trails in hydrothermal areas to prevent injury to yourself and avoid damage to the environment! Solid-looking ground may really be thin crusts hiding very hot water capable of causing third-degree burns and even death. Constantly changing landscapes make off-trail travel extremely dangerous!

FIELD NOTE: **GREAT GEYSERS!** Upper Geyser Basin contains 25% of the word's geysers and the largest number of hydrothermal features in Yellowstone. Over 150 hot water features are found here.

Find the trailhead in Old Faithful Village, north of Old Faithful Visitor Center and just before the Old Faithful boardwalk. Bear left (northwest) on the paved trail. (The trail to the right leads to Old Faithful Lodge and Observation Point.) Pass historic Old Faithful Inn and parking area on the left side of the trail. Stay alert as this paved trail, once an old roadbed, doubles as a bicycle path. Note that bicycles are not allowed on boardwalks.

Continue northwest along the edge of Yellowstone's caldera, into the Upper Geyser Basin. Pass Castle Geyser on the right side of the trail. Castle Geyser is the oldest geyser in the Upper Geyser Basin. Its fantastical fortress-like cone - the largest in the region - is formed by geyserite deposits. Castle Geyser erupts every ten to twelve hours in 90-foot (27 m) surges. Its water-and-steam cycle lasts about an hour.

At the boardwalk junction bear right to Crested Pool. (The trail to the left leads to Orange Spring and Daisy Geyser Group.) Crested Pool is a steamy hot pool that fluctuates between a slow simmer and a rolling boil.

Cross the Firehole River by means of a bridge. (Note the trail here is no longer wheelchair and stroller accessible.) Head northeast to Sawmill Geyser. Sawmill Geyser erupts every one to three hours in a propulsion of hot water that resembles a rotating circular saw blade.

Bear right at the trail junction, and on the right side of the trail see warm, murky bacteria-rimmed Liberty Pool. Backtrack to the trail junction and veer right to Spasmodic Geyser. (The trail beyond Liberty Pool leads to Geyser Hill.) Spasmodic Geyser erupts from a conical crater-vent every few hours in erratic fountain-like splashes up to 15 feet (5 m) high.

Continue north on the trail, and notice this basin's long-ago rhyolitic lava flows. The high silica content in these flows created blob-like mounds that crept across the landscape in strange forms. Bear right at the trail junction to Grand Geyser. (The trail to the left leads back to Castle Geyser.) Grand Geyser is the tallest, most predictable geyser in the world. Every 7 to 15 hours, Grand expels a fountain-like flow that can reach heights over 200 feet (61 m). Next up is nearby Turban Geyser. Its sinter deposits were thought to resemble turban headpieces. Turban's eruptions precede major activity from Grand Geyser.

Follow the boardwalk to Beauty Pool and Chromatic Pool. Beauty and Chromatic share similar underground thermal networks, which act in tandem. When one spring overflows, the other drains. Notice the colorful bacteria lining Beauty Pool's deep blue waters. These rainbow-hued thermophiles thrive in hot water environments.

Cross the Firehole River again via a bridge, and check out Oblong Geyser. Oblong is a major eruptor, pushing 10,000 gallons (37,854 liters) of water into the Firehole River every few hours during five minute-long eruptions. Next, meet behemoth Giant Geyser, the second largest geyser in the world. Giant Geyser's steaming cone is formed from hard siliceous buildups. Giant Geyser's massive jet-like eruptions can reach over 250 feet (76 m) in height. Further up the trail is Grotto Geyser, a strange bulbous-looking creation. Its odd form is possibly due to geyserite buildup on ancient trees that once stood near its vent. Grotto erupts every eight hours to about 10 feet (3 m) in height.

At Grotto Geyser the boardwalk intersects with the bike trail. Take a quick left on the bike path and bear right on the boardwalk to explore the Daisy Geyser Group. At the trail intersection, bear left to eponymous Daisy Geyser. (The trail to the right is another bike trail.) Daisy Geyser, a cone-type geyser, shoots out angled 75-foot (23 m) eruptions every two to four hours or so.

Next up are Comet Geyser and Splendid Geyser. Comet is a small splasher with a large cone while Splendid is one of the tallest geysers in Yellowstone, with spectacular sprays reaching over 200 feet (61 m) high.

FIELD NOTE: **STORM SURGE!** Although difficult to predict, Splendid Geyser is more likely to erupt when a storm front rolls through the area and forces the barometric pressure to quickly drop. This drop reduces the boiling temperature of the water in the geyser's subterranean channels, which may then spark an eruption.

Past Splendid Geyser, the boardwalk transitions to a paved trail. Bear right and loop around Punch Bowl Spring, a roiling hot spring named for its bowl-like appearance caused by sinter buildup. (The trail to the left leads back to the main bike trail.) At Punch Bowl Spring, an improved trail leads south to Black Sand Pool and onto Black Sand Basin.

From Punch Bowl Spring, backtrack and keep right at the boardwalk intersection to meet the main bike trail. Pass Round Spring on the right side of the trail. At the main bike trail, bear left and pass both the Daisy Group entrance and the Giant Geyser entrance. Push further north on the paved path to hot pool group Chain Lakes.

Take the horseshoe loop on the right side of the trail, and view beautiful Riverside Geyser on the lush green banks of the Firehole River. Riverside erupts every 5 1/2 to 6 1/2 hours in a delicate 75-foot (23 m) arch over the river, sometimes glimmering in a brilliant rainbow. Riverside's upsurges last about 20 minutes. Fan Geyser and Mortar Geyser, also on the banks of the Firehole River, erupt in tandem in varying intervals ranging from days to months.

At the next trail intersection bear left to Morning Glory Pool. (The improved trail to the right leads north to Artemisia Geyser, Gem Pool, and Mirror Pool, and eventually enters Biscuit Basin.) Lovely Morning Glory Pool is named after the vibrant trumpet-shaped Morning Glory flower. Once exponentially more beautiful, Morning Glory's location next to an early park thoroughfare attracted garbage-tossing vandals to its waters. Debris has now clogged the hot spring and altered its water temperature, water circulation, thermal activity, vibrant colors, and bacteria colonies.

The hike ends at Morning Glory Pool. Retrace your steps back to Old Faithful Visitor Center.

Length: 5.6 miles (9 km) - roundtrip
Estimated time: 2 to 3 hours
Elevation change: minimal
Rating: easy to moderate
Challenge: hydrothermal area
Attractions: many geysers and hydrothermal features, including Castle Geyser, Grand Geyser, Daisy Geyser, Riverside Geyser, and Morning Glory Pool; self-guided trail; bicycling
Trailhead: in Old Faithful Village, just north of Old Faithful Visitor Center, bear left (northwest) on the paved trail past Old Faithful Inn and parking area
Coordinates: 44.460162, -110.830111

Castle Geyser © Andrea Hornackova - Dreamstime.com

43. Fern Cascades

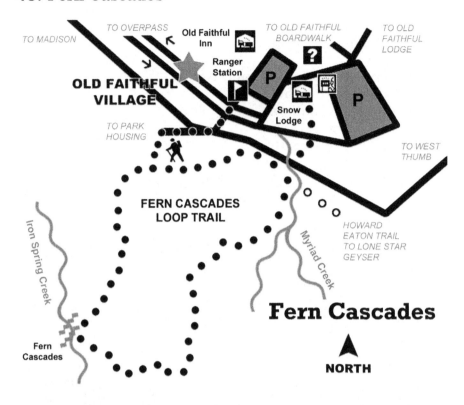

When the snow melts, a cross-country ski trail transforms into a moderately difficult 3-mile (4.8 km) roundtrip loop through burned woods to a miniature waterfall. Convenient Old Faithful Village access makes Fern Cascades a popular hike for Old Faithful area explorers.

Begin the hike in Old Faithful Village, by the Old Faithful Ranger Station. Follow a service road southwest across Old Faithful - West Thumb Road to a Park Service housing area. Southwest of the complex, look for orange trail markers that mark Fern Cascades trailhead. At Fern Cascades loop, bear right (west) to begin the counterclockwise hike to the cascades. (The trail to the left leads south to Howard Eaton Trail.) Follow the trail through wildfire-burned forests, and climb 240 feet (73 m) to the top of a hill. As the path levels out, find the cascades about a half mile (.8 km) from the trailhead.

FIELD NOTE: **WEE WATERFALL.** Fern Cascades is a tri-tiered waterfall flowing north in 70-, 20-, and 10-foot (21, 6, 3 m) drops down Iron Spring Creek. From the cascades overlook, the 10- and 20-foot (3 and 6 m) steps are visible but may only appear as rivulets during drier seasons. The lush ferns growing in the area give the cascade its name.

Continue on the loop trail, ambling over rolling wooded hillocks and descending back towards Old Faithful Village. In just over a mile (1.6 km) reach Howard Eaton Trail junction. Bear left (north) to return to the trailhead. (The trail to the right leads southeast to Lone Star Geyser.)

Length: 3 miles (4.8 km) - roundtrip
Estimated time: 1.5 hours
Elevation change: 240 feet (73 m)
Rating: moderately difficult
Challenge: 240-foot ascent (73 m)
Attraction: Fern Cascades waterfall
Trailhead: in Old Faithful Village, by Old Faithful Ranger Station
Coordinates: 44.457149, -110.832004

44. Lone Star Geyser

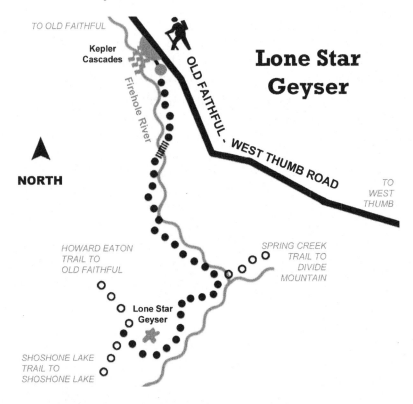

- Fat Ass Friendly - Multi-Mile Trail
- Attraction - Lone Star Geyser
- Activity - Bicycling

Grab your camera, time it right, and capture some juicy geyser action on this popular, moderately easy 4.8-mile (7.7 km) out-and-back hike to regularly exploding Lone Star Geyser. Expect encounters with bicyclists as this trail follows an old road that doubles as a bike path.

TRAIL NOTE: **TOO HOT TO TROT!** Stay on trails in hydrothermal areas to prevent injury to yourself and avoid damage to the environment! Solid-looking ground may really be thin crusts hiding very hot water capable of causing third-degree burns and even death. Constantly changing landscapes make off-trail travel extremely dangerous!

Find the trailhead 3.5 miles (5.6 km) south of Old Faithful Junction, at the Kepler Cascades parking area. Follow the paved trail south along the Firehole River, through pristine pine forests and across a bridge. Bear southeast (right) at Spring Creek to active Lone Star Geyser.

FIELD NOTE: **GEYSER RECORD.** Lone Star Geyser erupts every 3 hours for about 30 minutes. Its eruptions can reach as high as 45 feet (14 m). An on-site logbook keeps track of the geyser's eruption schedule.

Love Lone Star and return to the trailhead by the same route.

ALTERNATE RETURN: Continue on the trail, looping around Lone Star Geyser, to Howard Eaton - Shoshone Lake Trail junction. Bear right on Howard Eaton Trail, and follow the steep path 2.9 miles (4.7 km) through thick forests to Old Faithful.

CONTINUE THE ADVENTURE: Bear left on Shoshone Lake Trail, and hike 6 miles (9.7 km) south to backcountry Shoshone Lake and the 100+ thermal features of remote, pristine, and fragile Shoshone Geyser Basin. Shoshone Lake Trail also connects to the waterfall-adorned and wildlife-packed Bechler River region.

Length: 4.8 miles (7.7 km) - roundtrip
Estimated time: 2 to 3 hours
Elevation change: minimal
Rating: moderately easy
Challenge: hydrothermal area
Attractions: Lone Star Geyser, Firehole River, bicycling
Trailhead: 3.5 miles (5.6 km) south of Old Faithful Village, on Old Faithful - West Thumb Road, at the Kepler Cascades parking area.
Coordinates: 44.444531, -110.804638

45. Spring Creek

Spring Creek

TO OLD FAITHFUL

NORTH

TO WEST THUMB

TRAIL TO KEPLER CASCADES

OLD FAITHFUL - WEST THUMB ROAD

Firehole River

Spring Creek
SPRING CREEK TRAIL

DIVIDE TRAIL TO DIVIDE MOUNTAIN

TRAIL TO LONE STAR GEYSER

DIVIDE MOUNTAIN

A popular winter cross-country-ski trail and destination connector, Spring Creek offers cool respite in hot summer months on a difficult 3.5-mile (5.6 km) one-way hike through a refreshing canyon. Spring Creek is an excellent trail for ambitious adventurers seeking varied connections to Divide Mountain, Lone Star Geyser Trail, Howard Eaton Trail, and backcountry Shoshone Lake Trail.

Find the trailhead on Old Faithful - West Thumb Road, about 7 miles (11.3 km) east of Old Faithful Village, on the south side of the road at Divide Trail pullout. Follow Divide Trail north through thick forests to Spring Creek Trail. Bear right (west) on Spring Creek Trail. (The trail to the left heads south, straight up to the summit of Divide Mountain.)

Continue on Spring Creek Trail as it winds downhill alongside the creek, just north of the Continental Divide. Trace the edge of bluffs rising to the south of the trail. Hike a continuously twisting descent, passing a creek-side picnic area and occasionally hop-scotching over the creek.

3.5 miles (5.6 km) from the trailhead, Spring Creek tumbles into the Firehole River. Cross the river via a bridge, and arrive at Lone Star Geyser Trail junction. Pick your next adventure as the hike ends here.

CONTINUE THE ADVENTURE: Bear right (north) to follow the bike path up to Kepler Cascades parking area. Bear left (south) on the footpath to Lone Star Geyser. (See **44. Lone Star Geyser**.) Beyond Lone Star Geyser, Howard Eaton Trail travels north to Old Faithful Village. Shoshone Lake Trail leads south into the Shoshone Lake backcountry.

Length: 3.5 miles (5.6 km) - one-way
Estimated time: 2 hours
Elevation change: 370-foot descent (113 m)
Rating: difficult
Challenge: stream crossings
Attractions: Spring Creek, Lone Star Geyser Trail
Trailhead: on Old Faithful - West Thumb Road, about 7 miles (11.3 km) east of Old Faithful Village, on the south side of the road at Divide Trail pullout, just west of Craig Pass
Coordinates: 44.434804, -110.734821

FORGET IT, FAT ASS Hikes In This Area:

- ### Divide

Muscle up a mountain to the site of a former fire lookout on this 3.4-mile (5.5 km) roundtrip trek. Follow Divide Trail south, cross both Spring Creek and the Continental Divide, and scramble up 735 feet (224 m) to the mountain's 8,725-foot (2,659 m) summit.

- ### Mallard Lake

Escape the hustle and bustle of downtown Old Faithful with this difficult 6.8-mile (10.9 km) roundtrip trek over the Firehole River, beyond the bubbling mudpots of Pipeline Hot Spring, and through singed forests to Mallard Lake. This endurance tester boasts a 660-foot (201 m) elevation change.

- ### Mallard Creek

Work your calves on a 9.2-mile (14.8 km) hike to Mallard Creek, with a 920-foot (280 m) elevation shocker over hills and through scorched forests to Mallard Lake.

Fishing Bridge, Bridge Bay, Lake Village, Yellowstone Lake, and East Entrance Area

ROAD NOTE: Highways 20, 14, and 16 from Fishing Bridge to East Entrance (and onto Cody, Wyoming) are closed from early November until early May.

Fishing Bridge Area Highlights:

- Yellowstone Lake
- Waterways and Trout
- Grizzly Bears
- Geothermal Features
- Natural Bridge
- Mud Volcano

FAT ASS FRIENDLY Hikes In This Area:
(trail number and name)

46. Mud Volcano and Sulphur Caldron +
48. Pelican Creek
49. Storm Point
53. Natural Bridge ++

+ wheelchair and stroller accessible - in parts
++ wheelchair and stroller accessible - with assistance

NOTE: Wheelchair rental is available at Lake Medical Clinic.

Information:

Park Information - 307-344-7381

- Fishing Bridge Museum and Visitor Center

Fishing Bridge Museum and Visitor Center is located one mile (1.6 km) east of Fishing Bridge Junction on East Entrance Road. The museum highlights park wildlife.

- Lake Ranger Station

Located in Lake Village, Lake Ranger Station issues backcountry permits and distributes important park information.

- Bridge Bay Ranger Station

Located in Bridge Bay, Bridge Bay Ranger Station issues backcountry permits and distributes important park information.

Medical Services:

Medcor operates a medical clinic offering urgent care services in Lake Village during the summer season. Hours may vary.

Clinic information - 307-242-7241

Eats:

SUMMER ONLY
- Lake Hotel Dining Room
- Lake Lodge Cafeteria
- Lake Hotel Deli and General Store (groceries, restaurant)
- Fishing Bridge General Store (groceries, restaurant)
- Bridge Bay Marina Store (snacks, fast food)

THE HIKES:

46. Mud Volcano and Sulphur Caldron

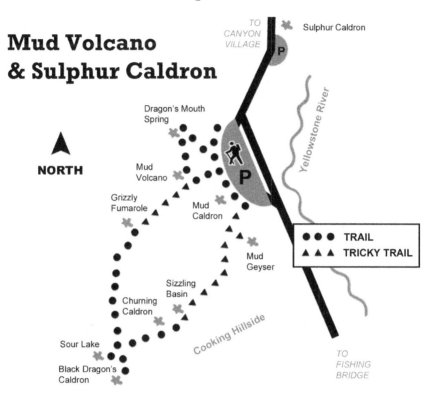

- Fat Ass Friendly - lower loop
- Wheelchair and Stroller Accessible - lower loop
- Self-Guided Trail

Behold! The smelliest place in Yellowstone! Relish the reeking stench of rotten eggs and sweaty gym socks on fascinating loop trails through the largest group of mudpots in the park. Mud Volcano offers short trails of varying difficulties that easily accommodate parties of multiple skill levels. Interpretive exhibits along both paths give visitors the inside scoop on the area's bubbly draws.

TRAIL NOTE: **STAY ON TRAIL!** Stay on boardwalks and trails in this area to prevent injury to yourself and avoid damage to the environment! Water and mud in hydrothermal areas are hot enough to cause third-degree burns and even death! They are also acidic enough to burn through shoes! Constantly changing landscapes and deceptively fragile ground make off-trail travel extremely dangerous!

Find the Mud Volcano boardwalk 6 miles (9.7 km) north of Fishing Bridge, at the parking area on the west side of Fishing Bridge - Canyon Village Road, across the street from the Yellowstone River. From the parking area, the northern-most boardwalk is a short wheelchair-and-stroller-accessible loop to intriguing Dragon's Mouth and Mud Volcano.

FIELD NOTE: **WHAT'S THAT SMELL?** Mudpots are unique thermal features where microorganisms convert earthy hydrogen sulfide gasses into sulfuric acid, which in turn transforms rocks into clay. Some gasses escape through the acidic, muddy clay and cause it to bubble. Hydrogen sulfide gas is the cause of Mud Volcano's noxious odor.

Dragon's Mouth Spring, a tempestuous, noisy spring inside a small cave, is one of the most notable Mud Volcano features. Watch this beast in action as water and gasses rush out of the cave's mouth while the orifice appears to belch and growl.

FIELD NOTE: **ANCIENT CREATION.** Dragon's Mouth is important in Kiowa creation beliefs as the beginnings of their Yellowstone home. The Crow people also hold the area sacred. They believe a young warrior changed a man-eating bison into Dragon's Mouth, which is now kept under guard by Mud Volcano, a cougar.

Continue on the boardwalk to Mud Volcano, a stewing pool of mud and gasses. In 1872 Mud Volcano was a violently erupting 30-foot (9 m) cone. It has since tempered down with the constantly changing landscape. An original portion of the stacks still remains, a survivor of a powerful explosion that destroyed the rest of the cone. The trail beyond this point navigates steep grades to Grizzly Fumarole and Sour Lake. Bear left at the junction to return to the parking area.

Explore other awesomely weird geothermal oddities on the left-most trail from the parking lot, on a clockwise loop. To the right of the trailhead is Mud Caldron. Notice its bubbling waters. Although the waters are heated deep within the earth, the bubbles are caused by gasses traveling up through ground fissures. To the left of the trailhead is Mud Geyser. Mud Geyser once erupted in impressive 50-foot (15 m) sprays. Thermal areas often experience volatile changes, and these days Mud Geyser is a roiling mud pit.

Follow the path south as it climbs up a steep grade through Cooking Hillside. Notice steam rising beneath fallen tree trunks. In the late 1970s, this area used to be covered with thick forests. Earthquakes, however, awaked thermal stirrings. This created 200°F (93°C) ground temperatures which roasted trees and vegetation until well done and dead.

Continue along the walk, noting the colorful thermophile mats of Sizzling Basin. The path levels out here and passes Churning Caldron on the west side of the trail. Churning Caldron was once covered with prismatic microorganism mats before earthquakes caused water temperatures to rise to 164°F (73°C) and the pool to spurt water 5 feet (2 m) high, effectively destroying the mats.

Beyond Churning Caldron is a short spur trail leading south to Black Dragon's Caldron. In 1948 this savage mudpot sprang to life in an explosion that uprooted trees and flung mud all over the place. Once a regular burster, Black Dragon is now pretty quiet - though churning beyond the colorful pool lining suggests there's still fire within the beast.

Backtrack to the main trail, and at the next short spur bear left (south) to Sour Lake, a lovely turquoise hot pool. Note dead trees jutting from its waters. This pool is filled with sulfuric acid and has a pH like battery acid. Beyond Sour Lake, and only accessibly by a ranger-guided hike, is Grumper, an enormous mudpot simmering in a super hot and super active hydrothermal area.

Follow the path north to Grizzly Fumarole. Grizzly Fumarole is an excellent example of the effects of seasonal and daily weather conditions on hydrothermal features. Depending on the amount of moisture in the ground, Grizzly may appear as a dry and cracked steam vent, a soupy mud hole, or a thick, heaving mudpot. From Grizzly Fumarole, the trail leads back Mud Volcano. Bear left to Dragon's Mouth Spring, or continue straight to the parking lot.

Before leaving the Mud Volcano area, be sure to check out Sulphur Caldron, just across the street by the Yellowstone River. With a pH of 1.3, Sulphur Caldron is more acidic than lemon juice and is one of the most acidic springs in Yellowstone. Sulphur Caldron's yellow pool churns with sulfuric acid and amazingly supports communities of thermoacidophiles (heat-and-acid-loving microorganisms).

Length: .7 miles (1.1 km) - roundtrip
Estimated time: 30 minutes
Elevation change: minimal to Dragon's Mouth Spring, 200 feet (61 m) to Black Dragon's Caldron and Sour Lake
Rating: very easy to moderate
Challenges: 200-foot (61 m) ascent, hydrothermal area
Attractions: Dragon's Mouth Spring, Mud Volcano, Sour Lake, Black Dragon's Cauldron, Grizzly Fumarole, Sulphur Caldron, self-guided trail
Trailhead: 6 miles (9.7 km) north of Fishing Bridge, 10 miles (16.1 km) south of Canyon; Mud Volcano is on the west side of the road; Sulphur Caldron is on the east side of the road
Coordinates: 44.624915, -110.433724

Sulphur Caldron © Svecchiotti - Dreamstime.com

47. Yellowstone River - to LeHardys Rapids

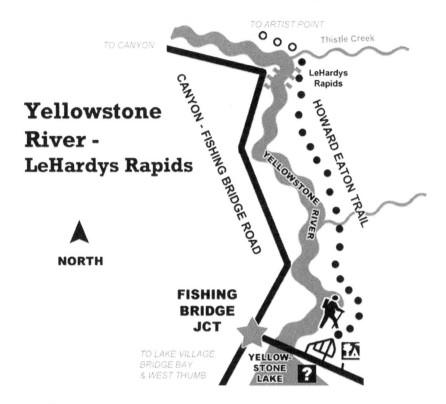

- Bear Area

Explore the true northern reaches of Yellowstone Lake along the banks of the Yellowstone River on this moderate 7-mile (11.3 km) out-and-back hike to an overlook of LeHardys Rapids. Along the way, experience a unique river - lake habitat that attracts diverse wildlife, including bears.

TRAIL NOTE: **PREPARE FOR BEARS!** This portion of Howard Eaton Trail enters a key bear habitat and may be periodically closed because of bear activity near trout spawning areas. Verify trail accessibility at Fishing Bridge Visitor Center. Use prudence, practice bear safety, and carry bear pepper spray when hiking this trail!

Find Howard Eaton Trail on the east side of Fishing Bridge, across the street from the Visitor Center and behind the service center, on the north side of Fishing Bridge - East

Entrance Road. Follow Howard Eaton Trail north along the Yellowstone River as it flows out of Yellowstone Lake. Pass a sandy beach on the west side of the trail and an RV park on the east side of the trail. Amble along the relatively flat trail, through sagebrush-dotted meadows and woods, while enjoying excellent views of the Yellowstone River.

FIELD NOTE: **ROCK-YELLOW-RIVER.** The Minnetaree people of Montana called the river, "Rock Yellow River" which French-Canadian trappers and later American explorers translated as "Yellow Stone." Ultimately "Yellowstone" became the accepted spelling for both the Yellowstone River and Yellowstone National Park.

Watch for bald eagles, osprey, and pelicans soaring over the river. The river - lake ecosystem, with its trout-abundant waters, is also an important habitat for bears. Keep an eye out for fishing grizzlies! About 2 miles (3.2 km) from the trailhead, hike through thick lodgepole pines; then, ascend 100 feet (31 m) over one mile (1.6 km) to an overlook of LeHardys Rapids, about 3.5 miles (5.6 km) from the trailhead.

FIELD NOTE: **YELLOWSTONE LAKE BOUNDARY.** Named for Paul LeHardy, a topographer with the Jones Expedition of 1873, LeHardys Rapids is considered Yellowstone Lake's northern geologic edge. At the rapids, the elevation quickly drops and sends the Yellowstone River flowing northward. In the spring, spawning trout leap upstream in these waters in an amazing feat of natural determination.

The hike ends at LeHardys Rapids overlook. Return to the trailhead by the same route.

CONTINUE THE ADVENTURE: The trail beyond LeHardys Rapids overlook continues north for 12 miles (19.3 km) to Artist Point Drive (South Rim Drive). Trail finding along this route may be difficult.

Length: 7 miles (11.3 km) - roundtrip
Estimated time: 2.5 to 3.5 hours
Elevation change: minimal, concluding 100-foot (3
over 1 mile (1.6 km) to rapids overlook
Rating: moderate
Challenge: bears
Attractions: bears, Yellowstone River, LeHardys Rapids
Trailhead: find Howard Eaton trailhead on the east side
Fishing Bridge, across the street from Fishing Bridge Visitor
Center and behind the service station, on the north side of
Fishing Bridge - East Entrance Road
Coordinates: 44.565256, -110.37478

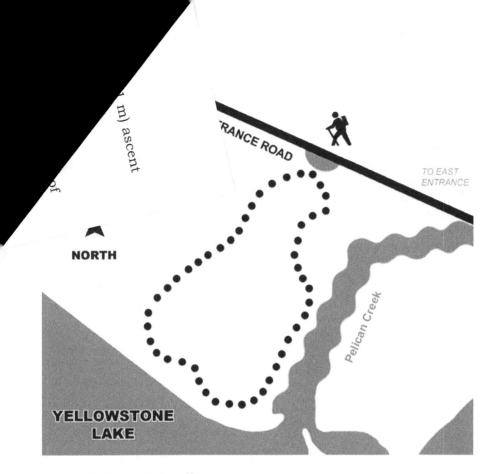

- Fat Ass Friendly

Embark on a world-class birding safari with an easy 1.3-mile (2.1 km) loop stroll through rich meadows and coniferous forests to the black glass shores of Yellowstone Lake and Pelican Creek. This short flora-and-fauna-filled hike also offers excellent opportunities to see big game relishing in the natural smorgasbord of a lush ecosystem.

Find the trailhead on East Entrance Road, about a mile (1.6 km) east of Fishing Bridge, at the pullout on the south side of the road, just west of the Pelican Creek Bridge. Follow the looping trail to the right, strolling along a boardwalk through boggy marshes and into a lodgepole pine forest.

In less than a half mile (.8 km) reach the black obsidian sand beaches of Yellowstone Lake. Take in expansive lake panoramas of Stevenson Island, Elephant Back Mountain,

and the Absaroka Range. Explore Yellowstone
following the trail east to the mouth of Pelican Cr

FIELD NOTE: **PARADISE OF BIRDS.** Trout-rich Yell
Lake   and   Pelican   Creek   offer   exceptional   bi
opportunities. Bald eagles, osprey, herons, trumpeter swan
geese, pelicans, ducks, and mergansers all populate these
waters.

Continue on the path as it loops northeast alongside Pelican
Creek. Watch for otters, elk, bison, moose, and grizzlies. As
Pelican Creek flows further into Pelican Valley, the trail cuts
back through wetlands and returns to the trailhead.

Length: 1.3 miles (2.1 km) - roundtrip
Estimated time: 30 minutes to 1 hour
Elevation change: minimal
Rating: easy
Challenge: bears
Attractions: Pelican Creek, Yellowstone Lake, birds, otters,
elk, bison, moose, grizzlies, Stevenson Island, mountain
views
Trailhead: on Northeast Entrance Road, 1 mile (1.6 km) east
of Fishing Bridge, at the pullout on the south side of the
road, at the west end of Pelican Creek Bridge
Coordinates: 44.560092, -110.360719

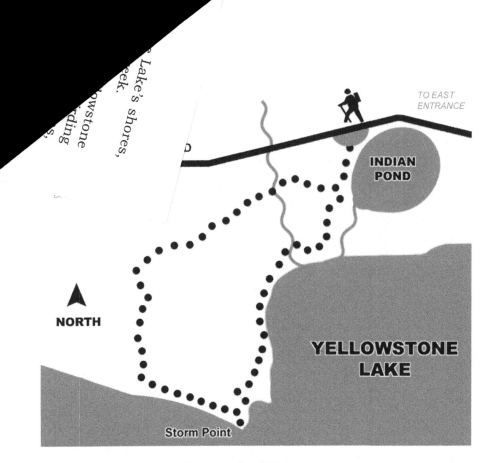

INDIAN POND

NORTH

YELLOWSTONE LAKE

Storm Point

- Fat Ass Friendly - Multi-Mile Trail
- Bear Area

Get swept away by amazing lake vistas on an easy 2.3-mile (3.7 km) roundtrip loop stroll to dramatic Storm Point. A trail of exceptional scenery traverses exciting wildlife habitats to a special outcropping on Yellowstone Lake, which is home to a colony of yellow-bellied marmots.

TRAIL NOTE: **PREPARE FOR BEARS!** This trail enters a key bear habitat and is periodically closed in late spring and early summer as grizzlies feast upon bison carcasses and gorge on trout spawning in nearby streams. Verify trail accessibility at Fishing Bridge Visitor Center. Use prudence, practice bear safety, and carry bear pepper spray when hiking this trail!

Find the trailhead on East Entrance Road, 3 miles (4.8 km) east of Fishing Bridge, at Indian Pond on the south side of the road. Follow the trail south for immediate, dazzling views of Indian Pond, Yellowstone Lake, and the Absaroka Mountains. Pass the western shores of Indian Pond, the site of a flooded volcanic crater and an old Native American campground. A few hundred yards from the trailhead meet a loop junction. Bear right to begin a counterclockwise loop. (The left path is the return loop.) Cross a footbridge over small stream and stroll southwest through a forest towards Yellowstone Lake.

Arrive at an open meadow teeming with wildflowers and waterbirds. Keep an eye trained for bison romping in the grasses and wallowing big indentations into the earth. Elk and moose also enjoy these meadows. Follow the path as it gradually descends south and east to a dramatic exposed bluff jutting over Yellowstone Lake. Marvel at the incredible vastness of this massive lake with its 131.7 square miles (341.10 km2) of surface area.

Bear right on a short spur trail to Storm Point, a rocky, windy weather-beaten outcropping on the lake.

FIELD NOTE: **MANY MARMOTS!** A colony of friendly yellow-bellied marmots have made their home in the rocky stacks before Storm Point promontory. Watch your step and you will see that these sturdy and adorable creatures are not shy at all!

At Storm Point, soak up incredible views of Stevenson Island and Mount Sheridan. On rare occasions when white caps aren't a'tossing, see thermal springs sizzling up from the lake water.

Follow the trail northeast along Yellowstone Lake's cliffs, and enjoy continually wonderful lake panoramas. Take a quick jaunt through a lodgepole pine forest, and cross a stream. Bear right (north) at the loop junction to return to Indian Pond and the trailhead.

Length: 2.3 miles (3.7 km) - roundtrip
Estimated time: 1 to 2 hours
Elevation change: minimal
Rating: easy
Challenge: bears
Attractions: Storm Point, Yellowstone Lake, yellow-bellied marmots, Indian Pond, bears
Trailhead: at Indian Pond pullout on the south side of East Entrance Road, 3 miles (4.8 km) east of Fishing Bridge Visitor Center
Coordinates: 44.559647, -110.326404

Yellow-Bellied Marmot © Alptraum - Dreamstime.com

Pelican Valley

- Bear Area

Prowl through one of the most outstanding grizzly habitats in America on a moderate 5.6-mile (9 km) out-and-back hike through beast-filled Pelican Valley.

TRAIL NOTE: **PREPARE FOR BEARS!** This trail enters a key bear habitat, is closed until July 4th, and is a day-use-only trail (9 am to 7 pm) with off-trail travel prohibited for the first 2.5 miles (4 km). It is highly recommended that you hike in groups of four or more people. Use prudence, practice bear safety, and carry bear pepper spray when hiking this trail!

TRAIL NOTE: **TOO HOT TO TROT!** Stay on trails in hydrothermal areas to prevent injury to yourself and avoid damage to the environment! Solid-looking ground may really be thin crusts hiding very hot water capable of causing third-degree burns and even death. Constantly changing landscapes make off-trail travel extremely dangerous!

Find Pelican Valley trailhead on the north side of East Entrance Road, 3 miles (4.8 km) east of Fishing Bridge Visitor Center, at the gravel road across from Indian Pond. Follow Pelican Valley Trail northeast through shady woodlands and open, wildflower-filled meadows. Gradually climb a small hill to a view of wildlife-rich Pelican Valley. Hike through the tranquil valley as the trail bends along the southern flats of blue-ribbon Pelican Creek.

FIELD NOTE: **BEST OF THE BEASTS!** Converging lake, river, and forest ecosystems of Pelican Valley create ideal big game habitats. In this diverse ecosystem, omnivorous grizzlies forage for plants, fish for trout spawning in shallow creeks, and feast upon bison and elk meats. Bison, native to this area (and having escaped rampant turn-of-the-century poaching), graze in the valley's grasslands. Wolves, specifically Mollies Pack, also roam this area, attracted by well-nurtured prey.

Hike northeast along the trail, and enjoy views of the Absaroka Mountains. As the trail bends slightly southeast, pass a small hot spring area. Remember, wandering off-trail in this area is prohibited due to fragile and hazardous habitats.

FIELD NOTE: **FLIGHT OF THE NEZ PERCE.** In the summer of 1877, more than 800 Nez Perce, resistant to resettlement on reservations and chased by the US Army, fled from Idaho and through Yellowstone, hoping to reach the safety of Canada. Their flight led them up Pelican Valley and across the Absaroka Mountains. The fleeing Nez Perce were stopped on October 5, 1877 after a fierce battle near Bear Paw Mountains, just 40 miles (64.4 km) from Canada. 39 sites in Washington, Oregon, Idaho, Montana, and Yellowstone National Park commemorate the flight of the Nez Perce as part of Nez Perce National Historical Park.

1.8 miles (2.9 km) from the trailhead, arrive at Turbid Lake Trail. (See **51. Turbid Lake**.) Bear left to stay on Pelican Valley Trail. In another mile (1.6 km) the trail branches at a ford over Pelican Creek and continues deeper into Pelican Valley. This is the end of the hike. Return to the trailhead by the same route.

Length: 6.8 miles (10.9 km) - roundtrip
Estimated time: 4 to 5 hours
Elevation change: minimal
Rating: moderate
Challenges: bears, hydrothermal area
Attractions: bison, bears, Pelican Creek, Nez Perce Trail
Trailhead: 3 miles (4.8 km) east of Fishing Bridge, at the end of the gravel road on the north side of East Entrance Road, across the road from Indian Pond
Coordinates: 44.559806, -110.318214

Turbid Lake

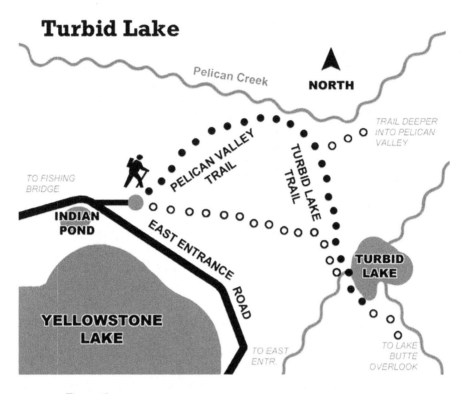

- Bear Area

Conquer the ultimate creep fest on a moderate 6-mile (9.7 km) roundtrip trek through the pounding heart of grizzly country. Prowl through Pelican Valley's bear-laden meadows to the muddy, reeking, carcass-strewn, burnt-tree-falling shores of acidic Turbid Lake.

TRAIL NOTE: **PREPARE FOR BEARS!** This trail enters a key bear habitat, is closed until July 4th, and is a day-use-only trail (9 am to 7 pm), with off-trail travel prohibited for the first 1.8 miles (2.9 km). Hiking in groups of four or more people is highly recommended. Use prudence, practice bear safety, and carry bear pepper spray when hiking this trail!

TRAIL NOTE: **TOO HOT TO TROT!** Stay on boardwalks in hydrothermal areas to prevent injury to yourself and avoid damage to the environment! Solid-looking ground may really be thin crusts hiding very hot water capable of causing third-degree burns and even death. Constantly changing landscapes make off-trail travel extremely dangerous!

Find Pelican Valley trailhead on the north side of East Entrance Road, 3 miles (4.8 km) east of Fishing Bridge Visitor Center, at the gravel road across from Indian Pond. Follow Pelican Valley Trail northeast for 1.8 miles (2.9 km) as it bows away from the southern banks of Pelican Creek. Hike through the grassy grizzly-and-bison-packed meadows of Pelican Valley. As the trail bends slightly southeast, pass a small hot spring area. Remember, wandering off-trail here is prohibited due to fragile and hazardous habitats.

At Turbid Lake Trail junction, bear right (southeast) onto Turbid Lake Trail. (The trail to the left leads further into Pelican Valley.) This rarely taken path meanders through grasslands, over wildflower-sprinkled hills, and through trees scorched by the 1988 wildfires. Descend towards the lake, navigating fallen trees and keeping a close eye on the fading trail.

Hike down a ravine and cross Sedge Creek outlet. Continue on the trail as it climbs the western shores of strange, sulfurous Turbid Lake. Here, crispy burnt trees line the shores, over a pattern of fallen logs submerged in the simmering lake.

FIELD NOTE: **MUDDY BUBBLER.** Turbid means muddy or unclear. The murky waters of Turbid Lake are caused by bubbling hot springs. The lake's crater was caused by a long-ago thermal explosion. Turbid Lake is very acidic and is incapable of supporting fish populations.

Off-trail explorations to the southeast reveal gurgling mudpots and steamy, sulfuric Turbid Springs sputtering near Bear Creek, Turbid Lake's inlet. Along the creek, see countless bear prints captured by the mud. Unsettling animal carcasses from grizzly feasts may also be strewn about. Remember to avoid remains! A nearby grizzly may want to reclaim its meal!

After tapping out at Turbid, return to the trailhead by the same route.

CONTINUE THE ADVENTURE: Beyond Turbid Lake, the trail continues another 4 miles (6.4 km), climbing and descending 500 feet (152 m) over Lake Butte to the trailhead at the Lake Butte Overlook side road off of East Entrance Road.

Length: 6 miles (9.7 km) - roundtrip
Estimated time: 3 hours
Elevation change: minimal
Rating: moderate
Challenges: bears, fallen trees, trail finding, hydrothermal area
Attractions: Turbid Lake, grizzly bears, bison
Trailhead: at Pelican Valley trailhead, 3 miles (4.8 km) east of Fishing Bridge, at the end of the gravel road on the north side of East Entrance Road, across the road from Indian Pond
Coordinates: 44.559845, -110.31832

52. Thorofare Trail - to Clear Creek, Elk Point, Park Point, Signal Point, Columbine Creek, Terrace Point, Trail Creek Trail, Mountain Creek, Thorofare Ranger Station, South Boundary Trail, and Bridger Lake

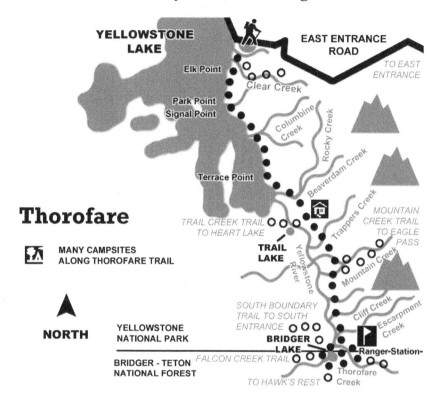

- Activities - Camping and Fishing
- Bear Area

Take a trek of a lifetime through the wild flora-and-fauna dreamscape of the remotest trail in Yellowstone. Thorofare Trail journeys a surprisingly flat 32 miles (51.5 km) on a one-way route. It explores the pristine eastern shores of Yellowstone Lake, meanders through the winding creaturous marshes of the Yellowstone River, and dives deep into the largest roadless wilderness in the continental United States. A spectacular summer hike,

Thorofare ventures beyond Yellowstone's southern border to secluded Bridger Lake, where an incredible outback stretches

30 miles (48.3 km) in any direction from any spark of civilization. Along the way, plenty of backcountry campsites and shorter spur adventures tempt more casual hikers. Thorofare Trail, at once a fisherman's fantasy, a hiker's paradise, a hunter's haven, and an artist's treasure box, magically captivates from the first step to the last.

A full there-and-back hike can reach upwards of 60 miles (96.6 km) and many hikers opt to complete their adventure with the help of an experienced guide and professional outfitting service. Most trail combinations require a shuttle (like a car) from the concluding destination.

BEFORE YOU GO: **CAMPING AND FISHING PERMITS.** Overnighters in Yellowstone's backcountry must have a Backcountry Use Permit. Campsite reservations may be made in advance. Bridge Bay Ranger Station is the closest permitting office to Thorofare's northern trailhead. Call 307-344-2160 or 307-344-7381 for more information. All anglers must have Yellowstone Fishing Permits. All Yellowstone visitor centers, ranger stations, and general stores issue fishing permits.

TRAIL NOTE: **SWIFT STREAMS!** In spring and early summer, streams become swollen and overflowing with snowmelt. Many streams on Thorofare Trail require logjam crossings. Fording these quick-moving gushers can be extremely dangerous.

TRAIL NOTE: **PREPARE FOR BEARS!** This trail enters a key bear habitat and portions of the trail may be closed until late July as hungry grizzlies flood the area to feast on spawning cutthroat trout. Use prudence, practice bear safety, and carry bear pepper spray when hiking this trail!

Find the Thorofare - Nine Mile trailhead at the turnout on East Entrance - Fishing Bridge Road, on the south side of the road, 16.9 miles (27.2 km) west of East Entrance Road and 8.8 miles (14.2 km) east of Fishing Bridge Junction. Follow the relatively flat trail south through wildfire-downed trees and along the eastern shores of ice-cold Yellowstone Lake. Think twice about jumping in! Summer water temperatures of this mighty lake rarely top 66°F (19°C).

FIELD NOTE: **ONE LARGE LAKE.** Like a vast inland ocean, freshwater Yellowstone Lake sports 141 miles (226.9 km) of shoreline and 131.7 square miles (341.10 km2) of surface area, and has an average depth of 140 feet (43 m). Massive Yellowstone Lake is the largest high-elevation lake in North America.

About 1.5 miles (2.4 km) from the trailhead, cross Cub Creek and bear right at the trail junction to continue south on the trail. (The trail to the left meanders southeast along Clear Creek.) 3 miles (4.8 km) from the trailhead, cross Clear Creek. To the right of the path, the lakeshore gathers at a projection known as Elk Point, so named for elk romping about this area.

Elk Point and its southern cousins, Park Point, Signal Point, and Terrace Point, are one of many famous fishing hot spots on Thorofare Trail. Yellowstone Lake has the largest population of cutthroat trout in North America. These lake points, along with the bountiful creek and river tributaries of the breathtakingly beautiful southeastern Yellowstone backcountry, shape an angler's Shangri-La. A fisherman's paradise, indeed: Just ask the grizzlies that bound here in spring and early summer to gorge on spawning trout.

Continue along the shoreline, and 6 miles (9.7 km) from the trailhead pass Park Point on the west side of the trail. Bear left to follow the trail along the lakeside to nearby campsites, or bear right to tromp through a marshy meadow. The two trails join to ford Meadow Creek and approach Signal Point. The mounts rising to the left (east) of the trail are Signal Hills.

Follow Thorofare Trail south through picturesque groves and meadow greenery. 8.7 miles (14 km) from the trailhead, arrive at Columbine Creek. Here, day hikers can catch a tour boat north to Bridge Bay. Slow boat speeds on the lake's Southeast Arm complement by-foot voyages along Yellowstone's peaceful waters.

Take note of Thorofare's well-worn trail bed. This historic route, with its easy grade and wide sweeps, was extensively travelled by Native Americans, trappers, and explorers of yore. Careful observation may yield clues of ancient dwellings under the prominent eastern peaks of Mount Langford, Mount Doane, and Mount Stevenson - all named for early park explorers.

Tracing the edge of the rugged Absaroka Mountains, cross Alluvium Creek, which is named for sediment deposits left by streams in river valleys. Alluvium Creek runs northeast where it skirts the northern edge of Brimstone Basin, a thermal area.

15.5 miles (24.8 km) from the trailhead, pass Terrace Point. Beyond Terrace Point, motor use is prohibited all together on Yellowstone Lake. Civilization fades to a memory as Thorofare pushes into the most distant and alluring areas of the park. Pass rocky cairns (mounds of rough stones), and 16.5 miles (26.6 km) from the trailhead, reach the Yellowstone River delta - the enchanting spot where the mighty Yellowstone River drains into the southeastern corner of Yellowstone Lake.

FIELD NOTE: **BIG RIVER, NO DAM!** The Yellowstone River begins beyond Yellowstone's southern boundary on Younts Peak in the Absaroka Mountains. It flows 671 miles (1,080 km) from its Yellowstone Lake inlet, past Fishing Bridge, through Montana where it leaves the park, and into North Dakota where it joins the Missouri River to meet the Atlantic Ocean in the Gulf of Mexico. Yellowstone River boasts the unique distinction of being the longest undammed river in the United States.

The great outback ahead unfolds in a marvel of open mountain meadows and glittering blue streams. Cross Beaverdam Creek, and trace the willowy eastern banks of the Yellowstone River as it winds through a wide, wet river valley festooned with moose. Watch for ever-present grizzlies and wolves that may be howling just out of sight. Can't-miss tracks from both beasts decorate the sandy riverbanks.

FIELD NOTE: **DELTA PACK TERRITORY.** The Delta Wolf Pack thrives in the Thorofare area, although Thorofare's remoteness often makes it challenging for Yellowstone's Wolf Project to monitor this pack. While numbers may vary from season to season, in 2010 the Delta Pack consisted of 4 adults and 5 pups.

Press south and pass Cabin Creek Patrol Cabin, which was built in the 1970s. 19.6 miles (31.5 km) from the trailhead, meet Trail Creek Trail junction on the western banks of the Yellowstone River. Bear left (southeast) to stay on Thorofare Trail. (Trail Creek Trail leads west over the Yellowstone River and along Yellowstone's southern shores to Heart Lake.) Thorofare Trail and Trail Creek Trail are the only two backcountry trails that traverse Yellowstone Lake's shores.

FIELD NOTE: **GRRR GRIZZLIES.** In the no man's land of the Thorofare backcountry, grizzly bears seem to galumph around every river bend. Naturally drawn to trout spawning in creeks in spring and summer, grizzlies have also become accustomed to feasting upon gut piles left behind by the seemingly endless trophy hunts of fall, just when the bears are instinctively fattening up for hibernation. The result is an increase in conflict between bears and humans, whom bears now view as their own personal gourmet chefs. Particular prudence when navigating these environs is a must!

To the west of the trail, note high-shelved Two Oceans Plateau, where precipitation funnels into either the Atlantic Ocean or the Pacific Ocean. Traverse rolling wildflower-filled Colter Meadow with its 10,683-foot (3,256 m) eastern guardian, Colter Peak. Follow Thorofare along the edge of the mountain, and cross Trappers Creek. The triple stars stacking eastward are 10,995-foot (3,351 m) Turret Mountain, 11,063-foot (3,372 m) Table Mountain, and 11,358 (3,462 m) Eagle Peak, the highest point in the park.

Continue south and cross Mountain Creek twice. 24.6 miles (39.6 km) from the trailhead, Mountain Creek's two trail entries run from the east (left) of the trail up Mountain Creek for 10 miles (16.1 km) to Eagle Pass and then into Washakie Wilderness. Bear left to stay on Thorofare. Enjoy Yellowstone's magical meadows as the river continues to wind through the pristine outback.

Follow the edge of resplendent Trident Mountain south, and cross a few meandering creeks before fording Cliff Creek and Escarpment Creek. Bear right at South Boundary Trail junction to stay on Thorofare Trail. [South Boundary leads 35 miles (56.3 km) east across Thorofare Creek, the Yellowstone

River, and Two Oceans Plateau, and through Yellowstone's southern outback to South Entrance Road.]

Revel in the sheer wild majesty of the Thorofare Creek - Yellowstone River confluence with its wild surprises and unremitting panoramas. 32 miles (51.5 km) from the trailhead, take a moment to revisit history by dropping by Thorofare Patrol Cabin on the left (east) east side of the trail.

FIELD NOTE: **WAY BACKCOUNTRY PATROL!** Yellowstone's backcountry patrol cabins were constructed in the early 1900s by the U.S. Army to accommodate troops safeguarding the park from poachers and other mischief-makers. These cabins were constructed about 16 miles (25.7 km) apart, which is a convenient one-day's travel. The cabins were all built in the Rocky Mountain Style with a covered porch and gabled end. Thorofare Patrol Cabin, built in 1915, is one of four cabins still used by the Park Service for backcountry operations in Yellowstone.

Bear left at the next trail junction to stay on Thorofare Trail. Follow the eastern bank of Thorofare Creek, and bear right at the next trail intersection to cross Thorofare Creek and begin the Bridger Lake Trail loop. (The trail to the left follows Thorofare Creek east to Petrified Ridge.) Leave Yellowstone and enter Bridger - Teton National Forest. Savor this remote milestone 30 miles (48.3 km) away from any road.

Continue through bucolic glacial meadows. 38 miles (61.2 km) from the trailhead, reach Bridger Lake. Bear right at the trail junction to explore Bridger's southern shores. (The trail to the left returns to Thorofare Creek.) Bridger Lake takes its named from famed larger-than-life early 1800s beaver trapper Jim Bridger.

Straight across the trail is Hawk's Rest peak. At the bottom of the mountain, Hawk's Rest Patrol Cabin sits on the beautiful marshes of Thorofare Creek. Bear right at the next trail junction to return to Bridger Lake, where the adventure ends. Select one of many returns.

Length: one-way to... Elk Point 3 miles (4.8 km), Park Point 6 miles (9.7 km), Signal Point 7.1 miles (11.4 km), Columbine Creek 9.8 miles (15.8 km), Terrace Point 14.5 miles (23.3 km), Cabin Creek - Trail Creek junction 19.6 miles (31.5 km), Mountain Creek 24.5 miles (39.4 km), Thorofare Ranger Station 32 miles (51.5 km)

Estimated time: days

Elevation change: minimal

Rating: moderate to strenuous

Challenges: trail length, stream crossings, bears, wolves

Attractions: Yellowstone backcountry, Yellowstone Lake, Absaroka Mountains, trout fishing, Thorofare Ranger Station, Bridger Lake, bears, wolves, camping

Trailhead: at the turnout on the south side of East Entrance - Fishing Bridge Road, 16.9 miles (27.2 km) west of East Entrance, 8.8 miles (14.2 km) east of Fishing Bridge Junction, at Thorofare - Nine Mile trailhead

Coordinates: 44.505715, -110.275537

Wolves © Mark Rasmussen - Dreamstime.com

Natural Bridge

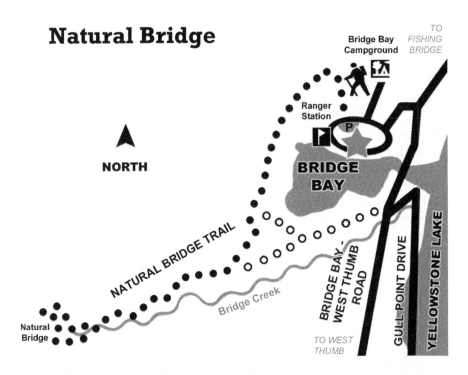

- Fat Ass Friendly - Multi-Mile Trail
- Wheelchair and Stroller Accessible - with assistance
- Attraction - Natural Bridge
- Activity - Bicycling
- Bear Area

Explore an unusual 51-foot (16 m) rhyolite arch on a moderately easy 3-mile (4.8 km) roundtrip hike along Bridge Creek to one of Yellowstone's most classic attractions, Natural Bridge.

TRAIL NOTE: **PREPARE FOR BEARS!** This trail enters a key bear habitat and is not open in the spring as hungry grizzlies fish for trout in nearby Bridge Creek. Verify trail accessibility at Fishing Bridge Visitor Center. Use prudence, practice bear safety, and carry bear pepper spray when hiking this trail!

Find the trailhead near Bridge Bay Campground, across the street from Bridge Bay Marina parking area. (An alternative paved bike path begins at Bridge Bay - West Thumb Road, on the southwest side of the bridge.) Follow the trail north alongside the campground entrance road; then, swing south away from the campsites. Cross a footbridge over wetlands on the west edge of Bridge Bay Marina, and hike through woods to a service road.

Bear right (west) at two road junctions, and watch for bicyclists as this portion of the trail also doubles as a bike path. A former stagecoach route, this road brought automobiles to Natural Bridge until the early 1990s. Continue hiking for about a mile (1.6 km) along a meadow bisected by Bridge Creek. Bridge Creek is a top-notch trout-spawning environment, so keep your eye out for hungry bears.

Keep right at the loop and arrive at Natural Bridge. The bridge is a fascinating 51-foot (16 m) tall rhyolite arch that stretches 29 feet (9 m) across Bridge Creek. A lone pine tree inexplicably sits the top of the bridge, gripping the moss-covered rocks with its roots. An exhibit at the base of the bridge greets visitors. In front of the exhibit, steep switchbacks lead up to the top of the bridge. Keep off the top of the bridge to protect its fragile structure.

FIELD NOTE: **BUILDING A NATURAL BRIDGE.** A determined creek tumbled over a plateau, seeping into the crevices of an ancient lava flow. As the water froze and unfroze, it chiseled away chunks of rock, creating this natural wonder. Early park superintendants proposed building a road over the arch, but luckily their plans were never realized, leaving this fascinating feature untouched.

Follow the trail as it crosses Bridge Creek and winds through a gully. Rejoin the main road, and return to the trailhead by the same route.

Length: 3 miles (4.8 km) - roundtrip
Estimated time: 1 to 2 hours
Elevation change: minimal, 50-foot (15 m) ascent to top of bridge, if desired
Rating: moderately easy
Challenge: bears
Attractions: Natural Bridge, Bridge Creek, bicycling
Trailhead: in Bridge Bay, across the street from Bridge Bay Marina parking lot, near the Bridge Bay Campground entrance road
Coordinates: 44.533877, -110.440483

FORGET IT, FAT ASS Hikes In This Area:

- ## Avalanche Peak

A barrage of difficulty waits to bow over hikers on an extremely challenging 4-mile (6.4 km) roundtrip haul to the top of 10,566-foot (3,221 m) Avalanche Peak. In addition to breath-taking panoramas of far-away summits, Avalanche Peak offers unpredictable storms, deep snowpacks into summer, a 2,100-foot (640 m) ascent over 2 miles (3.2 km), and grizzly bears feasting upon Autumn pine nuts.

- ## Elephant Back Mountain

This rump-busting 3.6-mile (5.8 km) loop hike, with an 800-foot (244 m) climb over 1.5 miles (2.4 km) through dense forests, rewards conquerors with 360-degree panoramas of Yellowstone Lake, Lake Hotel, Pelican Valley, and the Absaroka Mountains.

West Thumb, Grant Village, Shoshone Lake, and South Entrance Area

ROAD NOTE: Highways 89, 191, and 287 from West Thumb and Grant Village to South Entrance (and onto Grand Teton National Park) are closed from early November until the middle of May.

West Thumb Area Highlights:

- Yellowstone Lake
- Waterways
- West Thumb Geyser Basin

FAT ASS FRIENDLY Hikes In This Area:
(trail number and name)

55. West Thumb Geyser Basin ++
58. Riddle Lake

++ wheelchair and stroller accessible - with assistance

Information:

Park Information - 307-344-7381

- West Thumb Information Station

Located in West Thumb Geyser Basin, West Thumb Information Station distributes important park information to visitors.

- Grant Village Visitor Center

Located a mile (1.6 km) east of Grant Village Junction, on the shores of Yellowstone Lake, Grant Village Visitor Center highlights Yellowstone's relationship with wildfire and distributes important park information to visitors.

- Grant Backcountry Office

Open in the spring and fall months, Grant Backcountry Office is located .75 miles (1.2 km) east of Grant Village Junction, on the way to Grant Village.

- South Entrance Ranger Station

Located at Yellowstone's South Entrance, South Entrance Ranger Station distributes important visitor information.

- Thorofare Ranger Station

Located in the southeastern corner of the park, Thorofare Ranger Station distributes important visitor information.

Eats:

SUMMER ONLY

- Grant Village Restaurant
- Grant Village Lakehouse Restaurant (fast food)
- Grant Village General Store (groceries, fast food)
- Grant Village Mini Store (groceries)

54. Shoshone Lake - via DeLacy Creek

Stroll along popular DeLacy Creek on a moderate 6-mile (9.7 km) out-and-back ramble to 8,050-acre (3,258 hectare) Shoshone Lake, the largest backcountry lake in Yellowstone. DeLacy Creek's conveniently direct route to the lake often draws lots of midday foot traffic. Negotiate the crowds to earn a sweet peek into Yellowstone's sweeping backcountry.

TRAIL NOTE: **BITING INSECTS!** Wet creek areas and lakeshores attract bloodthirsty mosquitoes. Arm yourself with insect repellant!

Find the trailhead on the south side of Old Faithful - West Thumb Road, across the street from the parking area, about 9 miles (14.5 m) west of West Thumb. Follow DeLacy Creek south as it descends along a wide path at the edge of a lush, shady pine forest. DeLacy Creek was named in 1880 for Walter W. DeLacy, the first white man believed to cross through the area, circa 1863.

Cross a babbling brook and enter meadows brimming with summer wildflowers. Watch for sandhill cranes in marshy loam, as well as grazing moose. 3 miles (4.8 km) from the trailhead, reach the black obsidian northern shores of tranquil Shoshone Lake.

FIELD NOTE: **ROADLESS LAKE.** Shoshone Lake is the largest lake in the continental United States inaccessible by road.

Return to the trailhead by the same route.

CONTINUE THE ADVENTURE: Enter deeper into Yellowstone's backcountry, along two lakeside paths. Bear right (southwest) on the somewhat rough-and-tumble North Shoshone Lake Trail, and in 7 miles (11.3 km) carefully explore the fragile geothermal features of the Shoshone Geyser Basin. Bear left (southeast) to stay on the more-traveled DeLacy Creek Trail, and climb Shoshone Lake's steep eastern boundary to its outlet on the Lewis River channel. At the Lewis River, Shoshone Lake Trail branches right and heads west around the lake's southern banks to Shoshone Geyser Basin.

Length: 6 miles (9.7 km) - roundtrip
Estimated time: 2 to 3 hours
Elevation change: minimal
Rating: moderate
Challenge: bugs
Attractions: Shoshone Lake, DeLacy Creek, sandhill cranes, moose, summer wildflowers, Yellowstone backcountry
Trailhead: on Old Faithful - West Thumb Road, 8.9 miles (14.3 km) west of West Thumb, across the highway from the parking area
Coordinates: 44.446782, -110.701073

55. West Thumb Geyser Basin

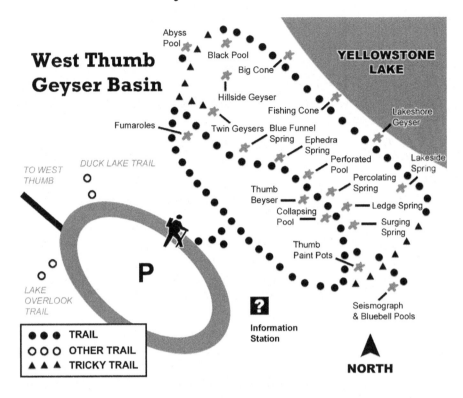

- Fat Ass Friendly
- Wheelchair and Stroller Accessible - with assistance
- Attractions - Fishing Cone and Abyss Pool
- Self-Guided Trail

Drift along the steamy shores of Yellowstone Lake on two very easy boardwalk and paved trail loops, past vibrant hot springs, seething mudpots, and churning sinter cones. The fully accessible inner loop is a quarter mile (.4 km) long and explores diverse hydrothermal attractions. The outer loop is a half mile (.8 km) long, has steeper grades, and travels among the lake-submerged cones and deep hot springs of this distinctive geyser basin.

TRAIL NOTE: **TOO HOT TO TROT!** Stay on boardwalks in hydrothermal areas to prevent injury to yourself and avoid damage to the environment! Solid-looking ground may really be thin crusts hiding very hot water capable of causing third-degree burns and even death. Constantly changing landscapes make off-trail travel extremely dangerous!

Find the trailhead at West Thumb Geyser Basin parking area, on the east side of West Thumb - Bridge Bay Road, a quarter mile (.4 km) north of West Thumb Junction. From the parking area, follow the boardwalk to the loop junction. Bear left to begin a clockwise walk around the easier inner boardwalk.

FIELD NOTE: **THUMBS AWAY!** About 174,000 years ago, a volcanic explosion created a crater that added a thumb to the larger hand of Yellowstone Lake.

As the trail bends to the right pass fumaroles, and at the trail junction bear right (southeast) to explore the level inner boardwalk loop. (The trail to the left heads northeast up a steep grade.)

On the left side of the trail see Blue Funnel Spring. Blue Funnel Spring is part of a network that connects Abyss Pool, Perforated Pool, and Ephedra Spring. Energy is transferred between these pools, and when one erupts, the others drain, and vice versa. In nearby Ephedra Spring and Perforated Pool, varying water temperatures and fluctuating water content affect how the features may appear at any given time.

Follow the trail to Thumb Geyser, which is inactive and buried by thermal runoff. Across the path is Percolating Spring, which once roiled and simmered just like a coffee pot. Next up is Ledge Spring, a hot blue spring on a shelf overlooking Yellowstone Lake. To the right of the trail see Collapsing Pool and its disintegrating edges. When full, Collapsing Pool is awash with rich colors. Continue on the path to Surging Spring, an active pool above Yellowstone Lake. The hot waters of Surging Spring regularly gush from the pool and flow out to the lake.

Follow the trail south to the junction, and bear left to Seismograph and Bluebell Pools. (The trail to the right loops back to the parking lot.) Keep straight at the outer loop intersection and see Seismograph and Bluebell Pools. These lovely steamy blue spools are named for the 1959 Hebgen Lake Earthquake that shook 7.5 strong on the Richter scale.

Return to the main trail, crossing over the outer loop intersection and bearing left on the inner loop to Thumb Paint Pots. Thumb Paint Pots are slurry-like mudpots with consistencies that vary with precipitation levels and ground saturations. At the trail junction, bear right to complete the inner trail loop and return to the parking lot.

Or bear left and begin the steep grade to the lakeshore features. Pass the Seismograph and Bluebell Pools spur to the right of the trail. Keep straight and follow the main trail as it levels out and bends left (northwest) along the lake. To the left of the trail, see Lakeside Spring, a warm, colorful pool draining into Yellowstone Lake. The blue-green tones of Lakeside Spring and its runoff channel are due to bright colonies of heat-loving microorganisms.

Continue on the trail and to the right of the path see Lakeshore Geyser. This geyser and its double-vented top are submerged under Yellowstone Lake until mid-August, when lake waters recede far enough to expose the geyser and its constantly boiling waters. Follow the loop northwest to Fishing Cone, a unique sinter cone protruding from the lake.

FIELD NOTE: **COOK-ON-THE-HOOK.** Fishing Cone was a big draw for fishermen of times past. Anglers would cast into Yellowstone Lake, and once they got a nice trout on their line, they would swing their poles around and cook the fish directly in the boiling geyser water. After many hot water injuries to the chefs and damage to the geyser cone, fishing is no longer allowed here.

On the trail past Fishing Cone is Big Cone, another large mineral deposit cone in Yellowstone Lake. As prominent as Big Cone is, it rarely erupts. The trail bends left here to Black Pool. In years past, Black Pool appeared much blacker due to dark thermophile mats covering the pool. In 1991 water temperatures rose and killed the dark-toned microorganisms, rendering the waters more translucent. Black Pool is about 40 feet (12 m) deep.

FIELD NOTE: **COLOR & TEMPERATURE.** Different types of microorganisms require different temperatures to thrive. Brown and green thermophiles generally prefer cooler water while yellow and orange thermophiles prefer hotter water.

Continue south on the trail, negotiating a steep grade to Abyss Pool and its earthy blue-green waters. Abyss Pool is one of the deepest hot springs in Yellowstone. It is 53 feet (16 m) deep. Follow the trail south and bear left at the short spur path to Twin Geysers. Twin Geysers is one geyser with two vents. Its rare eruptions are a spectacular show of two vents shooting out water splays to heights reaching 100 feet (31 m). From Abyss Pool return the main trail. At the next junction keep right to complete the outer loop, and return to the parking lot. (The trail to the right heads southeast along the inner boardwalk.)

Length: .25 miles (.4 km) (Inner Loop), .5 miles (.8 km) (Outer Loop) - roundtrip
Estimated time: 30 minutes
Elevation change: minimal
Rating: very easy
Challenges: hydrothermal area, steep ascents and descents on outer loop
Attractions: Fishing Cone, Abyss Pool, geothermal features, Yellowstone Lake, self-guided trail
Trailhead: .25 miles (.4 km) north of West Thumb Junction, on West Thumb - Bridge Bay Road at West Thumb Geyser Basin parking area
Coordinates: 44.415904, -110.573751

West Thumb Geyser Basin © Sally Wong - Dreamstime.com

56. Duck Lake

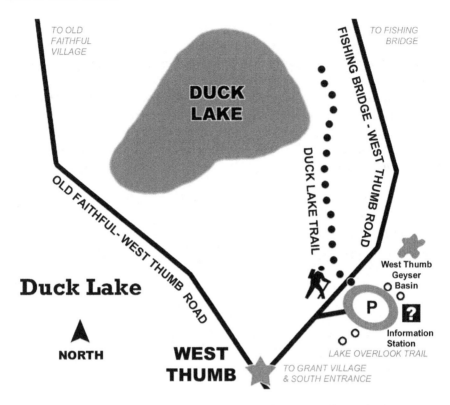

Waddle over fallen trees on a short, moderately difficult one-mile (1.6 km) out-and-back hike to Duck Lake. Along the way, explore an ecosystem bouncing back from massive wildfires, and see the aftereffects of a 10,000-year-old hydrothermal explosion on a peaceful landscape once rocked by violent forces.

Find the trailhead a quarter mile (.4 km) west of West Thumb Junction, at the northwest end of West Thumb Geyser Basin parking area. Follow the trail north across Fishing Bridge - West Thumb Road. Hike along a ridge, into a captivating checkerboard landscape created by wildfire. Follow the path through a tract of tall pines that escaped the ferocious 1988 Yellowstone fires. Pass a matrix of charred felled trees; then, climb 100 feet (31 m) over a half mile (.8 km) to the top of a hillock covered with small new growth pines determined to reclaim the land.

From the hilltop see a lovely view of 37-acre (15 hectare) Duck Lake shimmering beyond the pines, 100 feet (31 m) below the path to the northwest. (Sneak a little further east, on the opposite side of the trail, for a better view of West Thumb Bay.)

FIELD NOTE: **EXPLODING DUCK!** Duck Lake was formed by an immense hydrothermal explosion 10,000 years ago that forced debris out of the lake and into steep stacks to the west of West Thumb Geyser Basin. Look for volcanic evidence in the lightweight and porous pumice rocks strewn about Duck Lake. Pumice is created when frothy gas-infused lava rapidly solidifies.

Continue on the trail and descend through a dense forest to Duck Lake's sandy northwestern lakeshore. Although the lake is now fishless after past restocking efforts, ducks still bob about the waters. Explore the lake's peaceful beaches; then, follow your steps back to the trailhead.

Length: 1 mile (1.6 km) - roundtrip
Estimated time: 30 minutes
Elevation change: 100 feet (31 m)
Rating: moderately difficult
Challenges: 100-foot (31 m) ascent and returning descent
Attractions: Duck Lake, Yellowstone Lake
Trailhead: .25 miles (.4 km) west of West Thumb Junction, on the south side of West Thumb - Fishing Bridge Road, at the northwest end of West Thumb Geyser Basin parking area
Coordinates: 44.416318, -110.575038

57. Lake Overlook

A very difficult 2-mile (3.2 km) loop hike chucks intrepid hikers hundreds of feet up a lakeside hill to a prominent overlook of massive Yellowstone Lake and the snowy caps of the Absaroka Mountain Range.

Find the trailhead at the southwest end of West Thumb Geyser Basin parking area, at the orange trail markers. Follow the trail southwest across South Entrance Road and into a forest of mixed conifers, rebounding from the widespread 1988 Yellowstone wildfires. Watch for bears, deer, elk, coyotes, and the many different bird species that seek refuge in these woods.

At the loop junction bear right and cross a footbridge over a small creek. (The trail to the left is the return loop.) Continue on the trail through a usually inactive backcountry thermal area. Follow the trail west, and climb through a high meadow. Lake Overlook trail boasts an elevation change of

400 feet (122 m), so take your time and rest often.

About a mile (1.6 km) from the trailhead, arrive at Lake Overlook. Here, Yellowstone Lake dominates the landscape with sapphire-blue West Thumb Bay seeming to anchor the sprawling landlocked sea.

FIELD NOTE: **DOUBLE CALDERA.** Yellowstone Lake's main basin is part of the Yellowstone Caldera, a large volcanic crater created 640,000 years ago. (Yellowstone's caldera, at 45 x 30 miles, is one of the largest calderas in the world!) A smaller eruption formed West Thumb 174,000 years ago, nestling this crater within the larger caldera. Only July 25th, 1988, fire crews battling out of control wildfires jumped into West Thumb Bay to escape a raging wall of flames barreling towards them.

Beyond Yellowstone Lake to the east, note the peaks of the Absaroka Mountains. Look south beyond the Continental Divide to see the Red Mountains and 10,308-foot (3,142 m) Mount Sheridan. Complete Lake Overlook loop by following the trail down through meadows and forests. Bear right at the loop junction to return to the trailhead.

Length: 2 miles (3.2 km) - roundtrip
Estimated time: 1 to 2 hours
Elevation change: 400 feet (122 m)
Rating: very difficult
Challenges: 400-foot ascent (122 m) and returning descent
Attractions: Yellowstone Lake, West Thumb
Trailhead: in West Thumb at the southwest end of West Thumb Geyser Basin parking area, at the orange trail markers
Coordinates: 44.415429, -110.574722

58. Riddle Lake

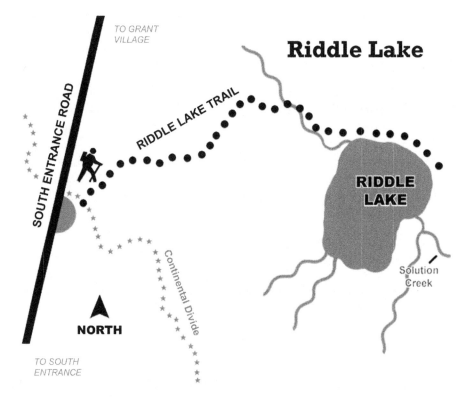

- Fat Ass Friendly - Multi-Mile Trail
- Bear Area

Decipher a natural mystery on this moderately easy 5-mile (8.1 km) out-and-back stroll through shady forests and serene meadows to peaceful Riddle Lake. Nestled below stunning Mount Sheridan, the sublime shores of Riddle Lake make a wonderful picnic spot.

TRAIL NOTE: **PREPARE FOR BEARS**. This trail enters a key bear habitat and is closed until July 15th. Hiking in groups of four or more people is highly recommended. Use prudence, practice bear safety, and carry bear pepper spray when hiking this trail!

Find the trailhead on South Entrance Road, about 2.5 miles (4 km) south of Grant Village Junction, at the pullout on the east side of the road. Follow the trail northeast across the

Continental Divide, and amble along a level trail that slips through a dense coniferous forest. Continue through lush, bear-perfect meadows, across rippling streams, and through moose-filled marshes. About 2 miles (3.2 km) from the trailhead, arrive at the northern shores of Riddle Lake.

Tucked below Mount Sheridan, Riddle Lake is a tranquil 274-acre (111 hectare) gem rife with cutthroat trout and dotted with lily pads. Stroll along the path as it contours the shoreline for another half mile (.8 km) to the lake's northeastern edge. Riddle Lake supports a diverse array of waterbirds like osprey, pelicans, and sandhill cranes.

FIELD NOTE: **SOLVING THE RIDDLE**. The Continental Divide forms the watershed that separates the rivers flowing to its east into the Atlantic Ocean or Gulf of Mexico, from the rivers flowing to its west into the Pacific Ocean. Early park explorers believed that Riddle Lake sat directly on the Continental Divide and named it for a lake whose water appeared to flow to both oceans. Aptly named Solution Creek, on the lake's eastern shore, solves the riddle - the outlet carries Riddle Lake's waters east to Yellowstone Lake and eventually to the Atlantic Ocean.

Revel in the riddle and return to the trailhead by the same route.

Length: 5 miles (8.1 km) - roundtrip
Estimated time: 2 to 3 hours
Elevation change: minimal
Rating: moderately easy
Challenges: bears, wet areas
Attractions: Riddle Lake, bears, elk
Trailhead: 2.5 miles (4 km) south of Grant Village Junction on Grant Village - South Entrance Road, at the pullout on the east side of the road
Coordinates: 44.358456, -110.581826

59. Lewis River Channel - Dogshead Loop

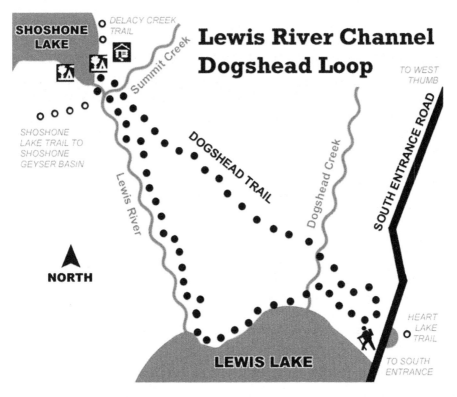

* Activity - Camping

The Lewis River Channel - Dogshead Loop is a difficult scenic 7- to 11-mile (11.3 to 17.7 km) hike through Yellowstone's backcountry along the radiant Lewis River Channel and up to Shoshone Lake, the largest backcountry lake in the continental United States. Lakeside campsites on Shoshone Lake are perfect for backpackers looking to add an overnighter to the adventure.

BEFORE YOU GO: **CAMPING PERMITS.** Overnighters in Yellowstone's backcountry must have a Backcountry Use Permit. Campsite reservations may be made in advance. Grant Village Backcountry Office is the closest permitting office to Dogshead's trailhead. Call 307-344-2160 or 307-344-7381 for more information.

Find the trailhead about 5 miles (8.1 km) south of Grant Village, just north of Lewis Lake, on the west side of South Entrance Road. Bear left towards Lewis Lake, and follow the path through big swampy marshes to the northern shores of the lake. Notice the hilly path follows an old lava flow. 2.5 miles (4 km) from the trailhead, follow the trail as it bends north along the eastern banks of the Lewis River Channel. The Lewis River flows from Shoshone Lake and is Lewis Lake's primary inlet.

FIELD NOTE: **A FAMOUS LEWIS.** Lewis Lake and Lewis River were named for Captain Meriwether Lewis of the famed Lewis and Clark Expedition. Most interestingly, while the Lewis and Clark Expedition explored territory within 50 miles (80.5 km) of Yellowstone, the expedition never entered park grounds.

Watch for elk, mule deer, and moose along this lovely stretch of river. Keep an eye out for osprey and other BOPs (birds of prey) that dive into the channel, fishing for trout. Take extra care in inclement weather as this area attracts bad storms and dangerous lighting strikes. The shorter hike ends at Shoshone Lake. Return to the trailhead by the same route.

For the longer route, follow the trail up to a small beach on Shoshone Lake, close to a ranger cabin and campsite. At the Shoshone Lake - DeLacy Creek Trail junction (see **54. Shoshone Lake via DeLacy Creek**), bear right (east) to continue the Dogshead Trail loop. Hike through a lodgepole pine forest scorched by wildfire, back to the trailhead.

Length: 7 (11.3 km) to 11 miles (17.7 km) - roundtrip
Estimated time: 3 to 8 hours
Elevation change: minimal
Rating: moderately difficult to difficult
Challenges: trail length, storms
Attractions: Lewis River Channel, Shoshone Lake, eagles, moose, camping
Trailhead: 5 miles (8.1 km) south of Grant Village Junction, just north of Lewis Lake, on the west side of South Entrance Road
Coordinates: 44.319972, -110.599526

60. Heart Lake

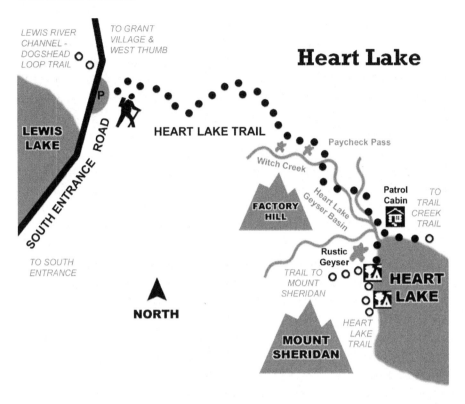

- Activities - Fishing and Camping

Feel the wild beating heart of Yellowstone backcountry on this popular, but peaceful, difficult 15-mile (24.1 km) out-and-back hike through big game heaven to pristine Heart Lake Geyser Basin and the vast trout-flush waters of magnificent Heart Lake. A gateway to Mount Sheridan and Yellowstone's tremendous outback, Heart Lake and its breathtaking backcountry campsites make an excellent overnighter for fishermen, mountain climbers, and enthusiastic explorers. A shorter 9-mile (14.5 km) hike crosses an incredible landscape to an awesome Heart Lake overlook.

BEFORE YOU GO: **CAMPING AND FISHING PERMITS.** Overnighters in Yellowstone's backcountry must have a Backcountry Use Permit. Campsite reservations may be made in advance. Grant Village Backcountry Office is the closest permitting office to Heart Lake's western trailhead. Call 307-344-2160 or 307-344-7381 for more information. All anglers must have Yellowstone Fishing Permits. All Yellowstone visitor centers, ranger stations, and general stores issue fishing permits.

TRAIL NOTE: **PREPARE FOR BEARS!** This trail enters a key bear habitat and is closed until July 1st. Use prudence, practice bear safety, and carry bear pepper spray when hiking this trail!

TRAIL NOTE: **TOO HOT TO TROT!** Stay on trails in hydrothermal areas to prevent injury to yourself and avoid damage to the environment! Solid-looking ground may really be thin crusts hiding very hot water capable of causing third-degree burns and even death. Constantly changing landscapes make off-trail travel extremely dangerous!

TRAIL NOTE: **BITING INSECTS!** Wet creek areas and lakeshores attract bloodthirsty mosquitoes. Arm yourself with insect repellant!

Find the trailhead about 8 miles (12.9 km) south of West Thumb Junction, on the east side of South Entrance Road, across from the northeast shore of Lewis Lake. Follow the well-marked, well-maintained, relatively flat trail east as it gently climbs over a rocky ravine for 4 miles (6.4 km) through young pines, grassy meadows, and pastel wildflowers sprouting up between fallen logs.

Trace the edge of the Continental Divide, leaving the Yellowstone caldera boundary behind. About 4.5 miles (7.2 km) from the trailhead, the trail opens up to a hot, shade-less plateau at Paycheck Pass.

FIELD NOTE: **FIRE TAMPERING.** In September of 2001, a small lightning strike caused a wildfire on Paycheck Pass. A visitor suppressed the fire. The Park Service was not pleased as fire management guidelines allow many wildfires to naturally burn. The action of this visitor was not only dangerous but may have seriously modified the Heart Lake landscape for many generations to come.

From Paycheck Pass take in a wonderful view of immense electric-blue Heart Lake sparkling in the valley below.

FIELD NOTE: **TWO "HEARTS".** "Hart Lake" was named in the 1800s for local hunter Hart Hunney. Later explorers believed the name to be homonymous "Heart Lake" after the lake's organ-like shape. This latter version ultimately became the lake's official spelling.

To the south of the trail, Witch Creek skirts the edge of the Red Mountains, with Factory Hill rising to a 9,601-foot (2,926 m) peak in the foreground. Along this upper portion of steamy, almost magical Witch Creek is the first group of hydrothermal features in Heart Lake Geyser Basin. From the creek banks to Heart Lake, five main hydrothermal groups contain hundreds of pristine, unstudied sinter-domed geysers, colorful hot springs, and sulfurous fumaroles. North to south, they are: Upper Group, Fissure Group, Middle Group, Western Group, and Eastern Group. Look for earth bleached white by minerals, and watch your step when exploring this region as fragile, unstable crusts often hide scalding water. In 1870 a horse from the Washburn Expedition fell through the delicate earth here and suffered terrible burns.

For an easy, pleasant stroll, stop at Paycheck Pass and return to the trailhead by the same route. For a more challenging trek with a spectacular reward, press on.

Beyond Paycheck Pass, a series of switchbacks descends 500 feet (152 m) along Witch Creek to Heart Lake. Open views showcase majestic Mount Sheridan and its fire lookout to the south. In this area watch for exciting beasts, their telltale tracks, and antler sheds. Heart Lake's warm hydrothermal pools, fresh water, and fish-packed streams create a veritable wildlife Mecca. Lumbering grizzlies, majestic moose, howling wolves, and grazing elk all roam this wild paradise.

About a mile (1.6 km) from the lake, the trail levels out and enters a lovely lush meadow just calling out for a picnic. Relax among the grasses and look for sandhill cranes gliding about this nirvana. A picturesque log ranger's cabin sits to the left of the trail on the final approach to the lake.

Past the ranger's cabin, the trail branches northeast and south. Bear left (northeast) to explore the northern shores of Heart Lake, and join up with Trail Creek Trail, a gateway to Yellowstone Lake. Bear right (south) to explore Rustic Geyser. This occasionally active spouter erupts in 50-foot (15 m) bursts for about a minute at varying intervals. Note the delicate sinter shelves of nearby Columbia Spring. These edges are formed as hydrothermal waters carry minerals to the pool's surface.

This trail also connects with Mount Sheridan summit trail. Most of Heart Lake's sublime backcountry campsites are located here on its southern shore and are popular with anglers and mountain climbers.

Heart Lake, at over 2,000 acres (809 hectares), is the second-largest backcountry lake in Yellowstone and hosts some of the best fly-fishing in the park. The lake contains native cutthroat and whitefish fish populations, as well as introduced lake trout.

FIELD NOTE: **FIRE AND FISH.** Although half of the Heart Lake watershed burned in the 1988 Yellowstone wildfires, it did not cause any observable changes in area trout spawning habitats or fish populations.

Heart Lake contains a spectacular array of birds. Canadian geese, loons, kingfishers, and bald eagles all flourish in Heart Lake's lush environs. Beavers are also active in the waters here. Ah yes, the lake's cool waters are mighty inviting after the long hike. Just be sure to wear socks or water shoes when taking a dip - small leeches have been known to hitch a ride on swimmers' feet.

After exploring this remote and wonderful lake treasure with its sandy shores and peaceful mountain reflections, return to the trailhead by the same route.

Length: 15 miles (24.1 km) - roundtrip

Estimated time: half-day to full day

Elevation change: 650 feet (198 m)

Rating: moderately difficult to very difficult

Challenges: 500-foot (152 m) descent and returning ascent from Paycheck Pass to Heart Lake, hydrothermal areas, bugs, leeches, little shade

Attractions: Heart Lake Geyser Basin, Red Mountains, Mount Sheridan, trout fishing, camping, wildlife

Trailhead: 8 miles (12.9 km) south of West Thumb Junction, on the east side of South Entrance Road, across from Lewis Lake's northeast shore

Coordinates: 44.317412, -110.598325

FORGET IT, FAT ASS Hikes In This Area:

- ## Mount Sheridan

Suffer a steep trail climb - nearly 2,700 feet (823 m) over 3 miles (4.8 km) to the 10,308-foot (3,142 m) summit of Mount Sheridan - on this demanding 23-mile (37 km) out-and-back hike. If you're not too busy begging for mercy at the fire lookout on top of the mountain, take in awesome southern Yellowstone views. As an added challenge, this trail will most likely be covered with snow until July.

- ## Pitchstone Plateau

The remotest of all southeastern Yellowstone backcountry trails pushes 16 miles (25.8 km) one-way far into Yellowstone's most unexplored wilds to furtive Phantom Fumarole and the world beyond, traversing a whopping 1,600 feet (488 m) over grasslands, lava flows, and the hard-to-navigate terrain of the isolating outback.

Trail Roundup

FAT ASS FRIENDLY Hikes

1. Boiling River 2. Fort Yellowstone 5. Lower Terraces 7. Wraith Falls	**Mammoth Area**
8. Forces of the Northern Range 14. Tower Fall	**Tower Area**
17. Norris Geyser Basin 18. Artists Paintpots	**Norris Area**
20. Two Ribbons 21. Riverside	**Madison Area**
22. Ice Lake - via Norris Road 27. Cascade Lake 28. North Rim of the Grand Canyon of the Yellowstone River - to Brink of the Upper Falls 29. South Rim of the Grand Canyon of the Yellowstone River - Artist Point to Sublime Point	**Canyon Area**

31. Nez Perce Creek - to Cowan Creek
33. Lower Geyser Basin - Fountain Paint Pot
34. Midway Geyser Basin - Grand Prismatic Spring
35. Fairy Falls
36. Biscuit Basin
37. Mystic Falls
38. Black Sand Basin
39. Old Faithful Loop
41. Geyser Hill
42. Upper Geyser Basin
44. Lone Star Geyser

Old Faithful

Area

46. Mud Volcano and Sulphur Caldron
48. Pelican Creek
49. Storm Point
53. Natural Bridge

Fishing Bridge

Area

55. West Thumb Geyser Basin
58. Riddle Lake

West Thumb

Area

Accessible Hikes

2. Fort Yellowstone 5. Lower Terraces	**Mammoth Area**
8. Forces of the Northern Range 14. Tower Fall	**Tower Area**
18. Artists Paintpots	**Norris Area**
20. Two Ribbons	**Madison Area**
33. Lower Geyser Basin - Fountain Paint Pot 34. Midway Geyser Basin - Grand Prismatic Spring 36. Biscuit Basin 38. Black Sand Basin 39. Old Faithful Loop 42. Upper Geyser Basin	**Old Faithful Area**
46. Mud Volcano and Sulphur Caldron 53. Natural Bridge	**Fishing Bridge Area**
55. West Thumb Geyser Basin	**West Thumb Area**

Self-Guided Hikes

2. Fort Yellowstone 5. Lower Terraces	**Mammoth Area**
8. Forces of the Northern Range	**Tower Area**
17. Norris Geyser Basin - Porcelain Basin and Back Basin Loop	**Norris Area**
20. Two Ribbons	**Madison Area**
28. North Rim of the Grand Canyon of the Yellowstone River 29. South Rim of the Grand Canyon of the Yellowstone River	**Canyon Area**
33. Lower Geyser Basin - Fountain Paint Pot 34. Midway Geyser Basin - Grand Prismatic Spring 36. Biscuit Basin 38. Black Sand Basin 39. Old Faithful Loop 41. Geyser Hill 42. Upper Geyser Basin	**Old Faithful Area**
46. Mud Volcano and Sulphur Caldron	**Fishing Bridge Area**
55. West Thumb Geyser Basin	**West Thumb Area**

FORGET IT, FAT ASS Hikes

• Lava Creek Canyon • Sepulcher Mountain • Bunsen Peak • Osprey Falls • Rescue Creek • Blacktail Deer Creek	**Mammoth Area**
• Pebble Creek • Petrified Trees • Specimen Ridge • Hellroaring • Mount Washburn	**Tower Area**
• Monument Geyser Basin • Mount Holmes	**Norris Area**
• Purple Mountain	**Madison Area**
• Observation Peak • Seven Mile Hole • Uncle Tom's Trail • Brink of the Lower Falls • Mary Mountain	**Canyon Area**
• Divide • Mallard Lake • Mallard Creek	**Old Faithful Area**

- Avalanche Peak
- Elephant Back Mountain

Fishing Bridge Area

- Mount Sheridan
- Pitchstone Plateau

West Thumb Area

Index

Made in United States
North Haven, CT
02 September 2022

23618863R00147